RESULTS
REVOLUTION

RESULTS
REVOLUTION
Achieving What Matters Most
FOR YOUR **TEAM**, YOUR **COMPANY**, YOUR **LIFE**

CRAIG HICKMAN   CRAIG MORGAN

Partners In Leadership®
Temecula, CA

This book is a work of fiction. Though some names, characters, incidents, and dialogues are based on historical record, the work as a whole is a product of the authors' seasoned imaginations. The foremost reality is that the authors have connected the fundamental principles and perspectives described in these chapters based on several decades of successful strategy, culture and leadership development consulting with many of the finest companies in the world.

Published by
Partners In Leadership
27555 Ynez Road, Suite 300
Temecula CA 92590
www.partnersinleadership.com
800-504-6070

Publisher's Cataloging in Publication Data
is available by contacting Partners In Leadership

ISBN13: 978-0-9980200-0-6

Dust jacket design by Pete Theodore
Interior illustrations by Sara Dwyer Design, LLC

Printed in the United State of America

21 20 19 18 17 • 5 4 3 2 1

To Laura, Winston, Bill, and Lorraine

CONTENTS

Preface

RESULTS ARE EVERYTHING

For the past forty years we have worked independently as management consultants and organizational change agents to help our respective clients improve their results. During these four decades, there has been a deluge of business books and management programs promoting all sorts of new approaches and methods to improve business results. In fact, we have written and developed some of those books and programs ourselves. So, it's natural and necessary for us to ask, "Have business organizations markedly improved over the past four decades?" Our answer, based on research and experience, is, "Yes, some have. However, only 12% (or 60 companies) from the Fortune 500 in 1955 remain today under the same name."

At the same time, in a majority of cases, performance

improvements achieved have fallen short of the promises made by authors, management gurus, program developers, consultants, trainers, or the business leaders who hired and espoused them. Why? The lamentable, hard-to-accept reality is that most business leaders and their countless consultants (including us) have been focusing all of our attention on the process rather than the prize.

As counterintuitive as it may seem, after forty long years, we have decisively realized, separately and together, that achieving business success is less about managing how we want people to act and think and feel in order to deliver the desired results and more about managing how we want people to act and think and feel about the desired results themselves.

Rigorous adherence to the best management and leadership practices does not always produce the needed results. In the end, business success always comes from people who clearly understand what matters most to the business, actively connect what matters most to the business with what matters most to them individually, and never stop working until they make all of it happen—plain and simple.

When people willingly commit to delivering a blend of what matters most to the business and what matters most to themselves individually, amazing accomplishments and incredible advancements follow, every time. That's why we've joined forces to write this book.

In 1975, political activist and management pundit Richard Cornuelle ominously wrote in his book, *De-Managing America: The Final Revolution*, "Management which manages by specifying behavior is dehumanizing and inefficient. Management which specifies results is emancipating." We have largely ignored and underappreciated Cornuelle's warning and are now in need of a Results Revolution more than ever. But first, we need to ask some important *why* questions? Why hasn't such a revolution already happened? Why are we still obsessing over behavioral change? Why haven't we learned to create genuine results partnerships in business organizations—partnerships that foster real commitment and determination to achieve joint results? Even the latest research on how our brains function, which is exciting and enlightening, begs the same logical question: why don't we care more about each other's professional and personal success in direct pursuit of organizational results?

We think the answers to these questions lie in the simple wisdom of an ancient folktale and cherished childhood story: *The Little Red Hen.* Yes, the little red hen produced an amazingly successful Results Revolution by closing the gap between expectations and outcomes. We call upon this classic fable of the little red hen throughout the book to help explain how one company used a simple regimen for managing and leading results to drive greater focus, energy, and solutions . . . and thereby achieved extraordinary results. Applying the story's elegant simplicity and enduring wisdom to today's creeping complexity and debilitating disengagement in organizations allows you to deliver unprecedented levels of results for the benefit of customers, shareholders, the organization, coworkers, and yourself.

Revolutionizing the way we lead people and results not only liberates and transcends, it also dramatically intensifies focus, expands energy, and speeds solutions, which transforms and guides strategy, leadership, and culture. This is exactly what we need. Today's business enterprises demand unrelenting improvements in results, because their customers demand them and their competitors deliver them. Along with this escalating demand and delivery comes an incessant pressure to reduce the costs and resources associated with finding better, faster, and cheaper solutions. Despite this persistent drone, great companies with outstanding talent often fail to deliver the expected and needed results. How does that happen? Enterprises and employees are currently trapped in a flawed *cause and effect* paradigm that increases rather than diminishes the distractions that hinder and impede the achievement of results.

In the pages that follow, we will not only debunk this half-century old pattern of management and leadership, but also provide a new pattern that takes full advantage of everything leaders and organizations have learned during this same time period.

To get there, we need a Results Revolution. Achieving and sustaining success in today's business environment requires different solutions—namely, the willingness and ability to change the way we manage and lead results at the organization, team, position, and personal levels. Whether in an orchestra pit, art gallery, sports arena, classroom, factory, customer's office, cubicle farm, virtual team, or C-suite, results are always going to be the key to success and those results always come from people who passionately want and need to achieve them. Sweet and simple . . . but we've lost sight and touch with these fundamental truths. It's time for us to reconnect and revolutionize.

We hope you enjoy reading this book as much as we enjoyed writing it. We also hope it engages your heart, mind, body, and soul, persuading you, no matter what your level in the organization, to begin creating a Results Revolution in your team and workplace today.

The Authors

1

DISAPPOINTING RESULTS

The torment was in the uncertainty—the lack of predictability, the recent setbacks, the gut aches. Three CEOs in seven years and now he was searching for a fourth to stem the tide of what had resulted in ten straight quarters of nagging little losses that were now packing a cumulative wallop. For Rogers, it had been agony heaped upon agony with no turnaround in sight. Rumors on Wall Street were raging. Employees either avoided eye contact or hid behind closed doors whenever he was around. The company's leaders were on edge, networking with their favorite headhunters while wondering what was coming next. Corporate cynicism had reached an apex.

Rogers Barrington, Chairman of the Board and grandson to the company's founder, sat in his stylish office on the 54th floor of the John Hancock Building overlooking a frozen Lake Michigan. It had been one of Chicago's worst winters on record, which to Rogers mirrored the company's dreadful performance. He was guiltily grateful that his office was no longer located at corporate headquarters in the suburbs. Making eye contact with employees had also become difficult for him.

At age 67, Rogers Barrington looked physically fit and notably distinguished—the epitome of a successful corporate leader—but he was suffering from heart disease. His doctors told him that if he didn't reduce the stress, he'd have another heart attack within two years. He hadn't even told his wife yet. Personally returning to the pressure-cooker role of CEO was obviously out of the question. Twenty years at the helm had been more than enough. Besides, he'd already made his mark with an impressive track record of taking his grandfather's successful business to number 598 on the Fortune 1000 list.

Despite his anguish over the company's recent failures, his heart disease was reasonably stable thanks to stints and medication and he wanted to keep it that way for as long as he could. Seven years earlier, he'd relinquished his CEO position and assumed the role of Chairman of the Board. But the company's current performance was aggravating a blood pressure problem. His doctor, wife, and family were imploring him to let go . . . *let go, right? Sure,* he thought, *just let go—how in God's name do I do that?*

The idea of *completely letting go* reverberated in his head, making his gut ache. This company wasn't just his life; it was a third-generation dynasty. His father had taken his turn at the helm. He had been a steady state player--just enough growth to keep everyone happy and next year possible. When Rogers Barrington took over, he literally changed the lives of every member of his burgeoning extended family and thousands of employees. In a million incalculable ways, he really lit it up . . . and it had to continue.

He cringed as he cycled back for what seemed like the zillionth time. A flurry of issues descended on him like a plague of voracious locusts. *All of this trouble started on my watch.* The typically reserved, buttoned up senior leader would never utter such blasphemous words in public, but the phrase resounded in his head along with the image of his grandfather's beet-red face.

Adding insult to injury, Wall Street was having a field day with Rogers' reputation and legacy. The painful but predictable gossip in competitive corporate circles had unfairly suggested that his early years at the helm may have been a fluke . . . that he had inherited it, not earned it. Rogers' insides burned when he thought about it, and his outward appearance was beginning to show the effects. He looked like he'd aged ten years in the past five and he was a lot crabbier these days. He was not a good loser.

This is grandfather's baby, he kept saying to himself, *those Wall Street parasites have no sense of the loyalty, fortitude, and devotion required to keep battling the odds.* In one sense, it would be easy for him to sell the company and pay people to manage the resulting fortune. But whenever he considered it, he could hear his grandfather and mentor screaming in his ear: *what the hell are you thinking Rogers . . . you can't sell the company . . . so you damn well better find the right successor to restore the company's industry-dominating growth. I couldn't get your father to agree, but industry dominance brings you economic leadership, Rogers, which is everything in business because it allows you to invest more back into the business than your competitors. Don't ever forget that.*

The old man had made his grandson promise to preserve and protect the family's golden goose . . . from his deathbed, no less. He'd seen something special in his grandson Rogers, but he hadn't lived long enough to see what his talented blood protégé had actually accomplished.

Even now, the one thing that continued to replay in Rogers' head wasn't the heart disease or his doctor's diagnosis after his first heart attack twelve years earlier that bypass surgery wasn't an option. It was the punishing petition made by his grandfather over thirty years ago, a few minutes before he died. The words pounded in his ears: *never let the light of our family's resolve go out.*

Rogers grimaced. *How has the very thing I've grown up loving become a millstone? Is this the way it always is with family wealth? A blessing and a curse?* He winced as he thought of his son and daughter, neither of whom wanted to follow in their father's footsteps. Then he winced, again, as he thought of hiring his fourth CEO in seven years.

For the past several hours, he'd been mulling over three finalist CEO candidates while reviewing the company's latest financials. Barrington Corp had become trapped in a malaise of mediocrity. Two and a half years of operating in the red had thrown the mid-sized conglomerate into an organizational stupor and there was no recovery path in sight. Besides enduring three CEOs in seven years, the primary issues were antiquated business models, disengaged workers, an uninspiring portfolio of businesses, and complexity creep.

Sadly, the once high-performing Barrington Corp had become just another also-ran in jeopardy of tumbling into the quagmire . . . or worse, the inglorious abyss.

Major shareholders, many of them family members who together controlled the company's publicly-traded stock, were very unhappy. Some were even considering shareholder lawsuits. The company's stock price had plummeted over the past three years from a high of $119 to a mere $35 per share. And, for the fourth time in seven years, the board of directors was trying to find the right person to take the helm of this flagging ship.

The $4 billion Chicago-based company, founded seventy-five years earlier by the eminent entrepreneur John Rogers Barrington, started out as a kitchen appliance manufacturer under the brand name Lake Shore Appliances. In the years since, Barrington had acquired and integrated over a hundred companies ranging from construction products to consumer electronics to software to financial services to alternative energy. Ten years ago, the company was a rising star expected by most stock market analysts to become a blue-chip investment for decades to come. Today, the company seemed more like a hodgepodge of lackluster performers that had grown out of control. In point of fact, some of Barrington's companies needed to be divested, some needed to be expanded, others needed to be strengthened through new acquisitions, and still others needed to be smartly repositioned in the marketplace. The new CEO would have to address all of these business challenges decisively.

Although Barrington would have preferred elevating an internal player, there was only one viable candidate for

CEO from inside the leadership ranks at Barrington and that was Jack Grossman, President of the Consumer Electronics Business Group. But Jack, in Rogers' view, still needed development and seasoning. Jack's time would come if he continued to perform and mature. So, Rogers was going to the outside once again. And of course, the boutique executive recruiting firm Rogers had hired was promoting what it claimed to be an exceptional slate of thoroughly vetted CEO candidates. Each contender seemed to be highly qualified and undeniably unique. However, Rogers had already spent a small fortune on executive recruiting firms only to see Barrington's last three seemingly well-qualified CEOs crushed or confounded by the challenges. In truth, he'd looked at so many of these candidate profiles in the past seven years that they all started looking the same to him . . . except one. For some reason, that he did not yet fully understand, Rogers was drawn to Ann Strong.

He thought back to the first time they met for lunch at the RL Restaurant in downtown Chicago. When Ann walked into the dining room, it seemed as if everyone paused mid-bite to watch her weave through the tables. She was wearing a royal blue sheath dress and matching heels. But it was her hair that made people stare. A shimmering red, it almost seemed on fire. As she approached the table, Rogers stood to greet her. She shook his hand firmly in a double-hander, expressed her delight to be meeting with him, and graciously thanked the waiter who seated her. Her hazel brown eyes were alive and inquisitive throughout their lunch conversation.

Like the other candidates, Ann had acquired a pedigreed academic background and worked for marquee firms making her bones. She had a commanding yet compassionate presence, but what made her stand out from the rest was her demonstrated ability to get results. She had already orchestrated two smaller yet impressive corporate transformations and seemed hungry to make Barrington her next triumph. Although both of her prior companies were significantly smaller than Barrington, $600 million and $2 billion, their turnarounds had been relatively rapid and definitely dramatic in scope. As important to Rogers was the fact that the employees in both companies still revered Ann Strong. She seemed to have worked miracles, winning over even the employees most resistant to change.

The executive recruiter who was recommending Ann called her a natural change agent—a real visionary—who was uncompromising about results. This was clearly evidenced by her track record of performance as a leader at Procter & Gamble and Berkshire Hathaway and then as a CEO of two transformations. Some analysts viewed her methods as extreme, pointedly harsh and edgy, but no one was arguing with the results she produced. She'd turned business losses and slow growth into profits and significant growth in two very different industries. Board members from each of her previous companies had confirmed it. But it was the people at her two previous companies—the ones that sucked it up and made significant change—that seemed to be her greatest admirers. In a world where attitudes toward CEOs are mixed at best, these people were still gushing with passionate praise.

Could she really be that good? Part of Rogers thought the extreme praise might be hype, but the other part of him thought she just might be exactly what his company needed. She was stable, solid, and savvy. Not perfect, but clearly competent and driven. She was divorced from a successful corporate attorney in New York City, but they still spent family time together on holidays and special occasions. Neither had remarried. It was something Rogers had probed in their first interview because nothing was above scrutiny when it came to hiring CEOs. From the beginning, Ann and her husband's careers had always come first. The unintended consequence was that they had a marriage in name only. They simply lost touch, failing to understand, acknowledge, and respond to each other's dreams and emotional needs. These realities had eventually led to unspoken disappointment, disdain, and estrangement. They had two grown children, a boy and a girl, both of whom lived in the Chicago area and were gainfully employed. By all accounts, she had managed to hold her family together despite the divorce.

Rogers resolved to sleep on it for one more night. His late father had always recommended the practice prior to any important decision. But he tossed and turned all night and was wide-awake by the time the sun began to rise. *This has to work . . . if it doesn't, everyone I care about stands to lose a fortune . . . and I will be remembered as the idiot who led the company into decline.*

In the breakfast nook of a downtown apartment next to his office, Rogers opened Ann Strong's file one more time while sipping his morning coffee and watching the winter sun rise over Lake Michigan. He reflected on his three face-to-face interviews with Ann, smiling about her distinctive no-nonsense approach.

She had shrewdly sidestepped the headhunter's second-round of screening efforts and navigated straight to the decision-maker, Rogers Barrington, early in the process. She looked like any typical senior executive—well dressed, confident and charismatic. However, the resolve in her eyes and the self-assurance she exuded made everyone take notice. So, did her vibrant red hair.

In their second interview together, she had disarmed Rogers again by using the fable of *The Little Red Hen*. He replayed the story in his mind just as Ann had told it two weeks ago.

The little red hen lived together with a dog, a cat, and mouse. The dog napped on the porch, the cat slept on the couch, and the mouse snoozed next to the fireplace while the little red hen did all of the housework. She cooked the meals, washed the dishes, made the beds, swept the floor, cleaned the windows, mended the clothes, raked the leaves, mowed the grass, and hoed the garden.

One day while gardening, the little red hen found some grains of wheat. "Who will help me plant this wheat?" she cried.

"Not I," said the dog.

"Not I," said the cat.

"Not I," said the mouse.

"Then I will," said the little red hen.

Then the little red hen planted the wheat, watering and weeding the ground each morning until the wheat began to grow. When the wheat was ready to harvest, she asked, "Who will help me cut this wheat?"

The response from each of her colleagues was again, "Not I." So, the little red hen harvested the wheat by herself.

The same thing happened when the little red hen asked for help to take the wheat to the mill to be ground into flour, to gather sticks to make a fire in the stove, to mix the flour with other bread ingredients, to knead the dough, put it into the pan, and bake it in the oven. Each time, her colleagues responded, "Not I." So, the little red hen did all of it alone.

When smells from the baking bread filled the house, the dog and the cat and the mouse came running into the kitchen.

As the little red hen took the beautiful bread out of the oven she asked, "Who will help me eat this bread?"

"I will," said the dog.

"I will," said the cat.

"I will," said the mouse.

"No, you won't," said the little red hen. "I did everything required to bake this bread and I'm going to eat it . . . all by myself."

And she did.

After that, whenever there was work to be done—bread to be made—the little red hen had three very enthusiastic and energetic helpers.

When Ann had finished telling the story, she immediately launched into its applicability at Barrington.

"The fable of the little red hen is about activating people to fully understand how business results can reveal the results they want and need to achieve themselves. I simply don't think this is happening at Barrington . . . at least not at the level you need. If you and I come to an agreement, this will be my focus. Getting people to take ownership for results that they truly want and need to achieve . . . and it has to start with us. In other words, what matters most to you and your family, what matters most to Barrington in light of the current business challenge, and what matters most to me as a prospective CEO of this company? The fable of the little red hen is not only about getting results . . . it's also about capitalizing on reciprocity. To me, it's about investing in my own success as well as the success of my coworkers, my teams, and the organization."

"No argument here," Rogers had said as he shook his head.

What followed was a thorough discussion of what mattered most to each of them and why. Rogers wanted his reputation intact, his legacy assured, his family of shareholders satisfied, and his personal life fulfilled and happy. All four of those "wants" depended deeply on Barrington's "need" for growth, profitability, employee engagement, and market leadership. Those four requirements represented the essence of Barrington's current business challenge.

Ann wanted freedom to operate, autonomy to lead another bigger and better corporate transformation, a generous compensation package with the commensurate number of stock options, and the respect and admiration of her coworkers.

Their common bond, of course, was what mattered most to Barrington Corp as determined by the current business challenge. It would be the only way for both of them to get what they wanted.

"This is the sort of reciprocal partnership we need to embed throughout the company," Ann had said emphatically, "it's the secret to sustaining the little red hen's success."

"I could not agree more," Rogers had responded while smiling broadly. Ever since that second interview, Rogers had been thinking about results, reciprocity, the little red hen, and what mattered most.

He picked up his mobile phone to call Ann Strong.

Yes, she was still somewhat of an enigma to him, but it was time to make her an offer she couldn't refuse. The company's economic clock along with his own biological one was ticking—even though he'd decided not to talk about the latter with anyone.

2

LIFE LESSONS

"Getting this company healthy again will require three
things," Ann Strong said. Her confidence and certainty were
unwavering as she sat at the conference table in Rogers
Barrington's boardroom. "A total restructuring of debt and
equity, a dramatic yet selective increase in both divestitures
and the right acquisitions, and a fundamental shift in the
company's mindset relative to owning results."

Rogers smiled and nodded his approval.

"I'm going to focus on the first two for the next
several months, until we get a verifiable and noticeable
improvement in financial results. After that, I will turn my
attention to the fundamental shift in mindset relative to
owning results. By then, I'll know this team and these
businesses inside and out."

"Agreed. You have my full support, Ann." He was relieved. Just 30 days on the job and she was running to daylight, as expected.

"Thank you, Rogers. I can accomplish the first two results rather quickly through outside bankers, attorneys, and specialists," she said, smiling judiciously. "However, without all 30,000 employees committed and on board, I can't shift the company's mindset."

"Right," Rogers said, a little cautiously, because he wasn't quite sure where she was going with her last comment.

"There's both art and science to transformation. The science side is precise and prerequisite . . . think of it as the detailed line work in your Rembrandt," Ann said as she nodded toward Rogers' prized etching of The Return of the Prodigal Son that hung on the wall of his office. "First, we have to restructure, divest, and acquire. That's the science of transformation. It will take me a year to accomplish and I can do it with or without the senior team's involvement."

"Why wouldn't you involve the senior team?"

"Frankly, after three CEOs in seven years, the nine senior leaders reporting to me are more than a little uncertain and skeptical. They're also very focused on their own business groups and functions, which is perfect. They'll be watching me like hawks and I'll be watching them. Of course, they'll be involved in the recapitalization, divestitures, and acquisitions when necessary or when they want to be."

Rogers winced as he thought about the company's last three CEOs. The first one who replaced him had been left-brained and a consultant-happy recruit from the outside. On his watch, the world's best change management firms had descended upon the company like packs of rabid dogs.

Barrington was a veritable feast. Twenty-four months and millions in fees later, the consultants' so-called brilliant solutions were not delivering the promised traction or results. All of their make-good provisions had expired, and they were now long gone.

His second successor, the CEO who stayed the longest at just over three years, had been right-brained and a training fanatic. He trained everybody, all 30,000 employees, in communicating effectively, continuous improvement, strategic value creation, and delivering customer solutions.

Each new program became a surrogate religion with its own sermons designed to extract the required mindshare and heartspace from other activities while professing to integrate with everything that had come before. While the programs created learning and development, none of them produced the needed results and the company continued to falter. An alarming alignment emerged around two unspoken fears: *most of this stuff is never going to stick and we're wasting valuable time and resources trying to implement it.*

CEO number three, another short-timer at twenty months, had been more whole-brained and a marketing whiz who promised to revolutionize the company's digital and social media presence. Because of his efforts, SAP, ERP, CRM, DDD and a beautifully integrated corporate website were now a part of Barrington Corp. The shrink-wrap on this new infrastructure shone in industry journals while the company's financial results continued to spiral downward. CEO three had digitally rebranded the company while its product and service reputation burned on Wall Street. Thank God, the company's historical standing with customers, suppliers, and employees had been strong enough to keep the family's beacon from being extinguished.

Dissatisfaction among shareholders and board members had started to boil. To avoid mutiny, Rogers' trusted advisors urged him to terminate the third CEO. The company couldn't afford any more infrastructure enhancements; it had to produce results that met targets. Now!

That termination occurred three months ago, but it now seemed like a lifetime ago to the founder's grandson. Wall Street had characterized Barrington's revolving door at the helm as a gross failure in board governance. Rogers was ashamed. This failure thrashed him and his company more soundly and publically than the previous two. At times, he'd wanted to crawl into a hole and die. *It can't happen again,* he thought.

"Tell me about the art side of transformation," Rogers said.

"The art side of transformation is all about releasing and harnessing emotion and energy. Passion like the energy conveyed in your Rembrandt is essential. I need that kind of magical impact expressed through the senior team's genuine commitment, focus, and communication to shift the company's mindset . . . all 30,000 mindsets. I won't have any access to the release of their enthusiasm until they feel it themselves. And, yes, I believe it is more difficult for a woman leader to achieve that legitimate engagement from a senior team. So, let's think little red hen. Once they see me successfully restructure, divest, and acquire, they'll likely be more willing and anxious to help. The transformation of Barrington Corp will emerge from a blending of science and art . . . just as Rembrandt's timeless masterpiece emerges from precise lines and tender images."

"Thank you for the clear explanation," Rogers said, reflecting on Ann and his Rembrandt.

Ann's business acumen was complemented by her commitment to the success and development of others. She had figured out how to blend the two into extraordinary achievement.

"Now I'm dying to know how you're going to change the company's mindset . . . all 30,000 mindsets."

Ann leaned forward. "I hate to say this but, there's no real employee commitment to results in this company . . . and it seems you, myself, and the board are the only people who see the problem," she stated in a matter-of-fact voice. "Please don't misunderstand me on this point. Barrington's employees are generally very hard-working people; in fact, they are some of the hardest working people I've ever met.

"That being said, some of them are hurting us by underperforming and encouraging others to do the same. But that's not the biggest problem. The real issue is that a large majority of employees are focusing on anything and everything but the key results we need to deliver. It seems that they're feeling worn out and whiplashed from the past three leadership regimes and their accompanying inconsistencies and contradictions. As much as they seem to truly love the company, they don't feel the energy that comes from genuinely sharing in the firm's successes or failures . . . because they're detached from what matters most: delivery of the key results. Sure, they get paid and may get a profit sharing bonus, but they are not really experiencing true reciprocity and they never have. As a consequence, ownership for results remains at the loyal hired hand, transactional level at best."

Ann was a hard-nosed leader when it came to business but she loved people and always wanted them to flourish along with the business. Business success without people success was a hollow victory for her. What matters most to the people in the organization must also be part of what matters most to the organization.

"That's why you're here, Ann. To do whatever is necessary to get this company back on a path toward sustained, profitable growth." Rogers knew that what she was saying was true. His family's values around the treatment of employees were a core part of the company's past success. It had taken decades of blood, sweat and tears to build . . . but things were more tenuous and less predictable now. He reminded himself of what she'd done in her two previous companies.

Ann thought for a moment and then leaned in again. When she spoke, her words came out more slowly and deliberately. "I need to get everyone's attention . . . both leaders and employees . . . and then refocus it. But I don't expect it to be easy. This isn't about changing their behavior first. It's about changing their perspective relative to results first. Cause-and-effect. Only then, will they voluntarily change the way they think, feel and act. I want you to understand that it will be painful for nearly all of them in the beginning . . . as well as tough on you, the Board and the company's major shareholders."

Rogers smiled guardedly. "I am well aware of your track record and general approach to things, Ann. Your plan to use the fable of the little red hen to get people to take ownership seems fitting for us, and it's obviously worked before." He paused, smiling, more openly now. "As long as you don't trample on the company's long-standing values of integrity, fairness, respect, trustworthiness and customer service or start making wholesale firings, you have freedom and autonomy to get us back on track. Just remember, my grandfather's philosophy was to give every employee ample opportunity to improve before letting him or her go. His values cannot be disregarded . . . I gave him my word on his deathbed," Rogers said, pausing again, but this time there was no smile, just a look of solemn resolve. "Everything else is fair game. However, I do think that if you give our people a chance, the vast majority of them will respond."

"Wise promise. Your grandfather's values will never be compromised," Ann said as the two of them stood up from the conference table. "To be perfectly clear, the company's leaders and employees will have ample opportunity to grow right along with me. But make no mistake, if we're going to successfully address Barrington's business challenges, their hearts and minds will have to shift from *work hard* to *create value* . . . and that shift has to be something they choose on their own because of the results at stake. Don't take this the wrong way, Rogers. This is a great place to work but it's still a benevolent dictatorship . . . most companies are. We need to change that. Anyone who is unable to make the necessary transition to seeking out and creating more value will receive ample assistance to find another place to earn a living. Barrington's industry dominance and economic leadership are on the line."

Rogers' eyes lit up at her mention of his grandfather's watchful words. Even though she made him feel slightly uncomfortable at times, Rogers liked her. "Make it happen, Ann," he said optimistically but with a hint of uncertainty. He had been through too many disappointments to put his trust in plans or words. He needed to see real results.

The "prove it" tone of his response did not deter Ann in the least. *I'll just have to earn his trust right along with all of the rest.* "We *are* going to make it happen, Rogers, but I'll need your support with the board and the family . . . every step of the way. You get what you want, the company gets what it needs and I get what I want. That's how red hen reciprocity works."

Rogers felt her resolve . . . it was like his own. *Never let the light of our family's resolve go out.* What Rogers Barrington did not yet know about Ann Strong was that a singular experience earlier in her career had profoundly changed her perspective and her life. It was an experience that both revealed and ingrained in her a simple, fundamental truth: achieving results is the key to everything.

Ann's life-changing experience happened between her first and second years at Northwestern's MBA program. She was working for a small boutique-consulting firm under the direction of Ted McKnelly, a PhD industrial psychologist with a flair for business strategy and culture. Near the end of the summer, after several weeks of working primarily with one specialty chemicals client, Ann had become frustrated and discouraged by the client's slow and unenthusiastic response to her recommendations. Even McKnelly considered her recommendations brilliant. However, Ann's consternation over the situation eventually led to a long dinner conversation with McKnelly about business, careers and life in general. By the end of the evening, Ted McKnelly's message to Ann became more direct. It was a message she would never forget.

"So, what's the most important thing you've learned this summer?" McKnelly asked.

"I don't want to work for clients that ignore what we have to say," Ann said. "Why hire us in the first place if they're going to remain stuck in their old ways?"

"What if it's not about them . . . and it's about you?" McKnelly shot back.

Ann was caught off guard by his directness. She chose to remain silent for a moment as she took a last sip of after-dinner coffee. The comment had stunned her a bit, and she fumbled to ask, "What do you mean?"

"You have to create the desire for change in your clients, Ann . . . and you can only do that by tapping into their most crucial wants and needs," McKnelly responded.

Ann's mind began scanning what she might be missing as she waited for him to explain further.

McKnelly continued. "No client is ever going to implement your recommendations just because they're brilliant or perfectly logical. Clients implement recommendations because they feel the need to do so . . . because they want to . . . because they can no longer live without implementing them."

"Everything I recommended ties to the needs *they* identified," Ann retorted, her frustration beginning to rise.

McKnelly leaned over his plate, looking directly into Ann's eyes. "So why aren't they chomping at the bit to implement your recommendations?"

Ann thought for an instant about what she should say, but then her emotions took over. "Because they're incompetent and lazy."

McKnelly smiled. Then he turned deadly serious. "I'm going to give you some counsel that took me way too long to learn." He paused a moment to make sure she was ready to hear what he had to say. "No one is going to take care of you in this life."

Ann was both dazed and discouraged by the comment. She sat back in her chair to take a deep breath. She had worked long and hard on her recommendations for this client—recommendations that were precisely what the client needed to improve its results. *I don't need or want anyone to take care of me.*

When McKnelly saw the tears forming in her eyes, he kindheartedly shifted his direct and pointed approach by explaining his thoughts more compassionately. "You are enormously talented, Ann. Nothing is outside your reach in this life. Nothing, but that's only if you truly own all of the results you want to achieve!"

Making an effort to fight back her tears, Ann managed to ask, "What does that mean?"

"It means you literally have to own the outcomes that matter most to you. If you want your client to implement your recommendations, you have to take ownership for that end result. Which means you have to know exactly where your client stands and what's preventing your client from getting to where he, she or they need to be. If they're not embracing your recommendations, you have to address their lack of motivation—if you really want to help them achieve the results they claim they want to achieve. Learn to own the results you want and need to achieve, Ann, and nothing will stop you."

Ann just looked at him, trying to understand what he was saying.

McKnelly continued. "The more specific you get about the results you want to achieve, the more focus, energy and solutions it brings. If you want a client to adopt your recommendations, define what that looks like up front in as much detail as possible. What do you want the client to think and feel and do? What outcomes will the client achieve when they do? When will it happen? How will it be sustained? The only way you learn how to own your results is by making them extremely specific with clear "must deliver" targets. Then never let up. Stay focused, keep your energy high and always look for new solutions until you achieve the results you want. And that includes getting the necessary buy-in from everyone involved or it won't happen."

Ann still looked unsettled and disheartened, as though she was a puzzled child.

"Whenever I find myself not owning the results I want, and it happens to me more often than you might think…" McKnelly waited to see the flicker of hope in Ann's hazel brown eyes. When he saw it, he continued, "…that's when I think about the little red hen."

"The children's story?" Ann said, somewhat defensively. She had no desire to be patronized.

"It's much more than a children's story. My mother, like most mothers I suppose, taught me that it was a lesson in sharing. I've since learned it's a lesson in leadership."

The natural inquisitiveness in Ann's eyes returned as she said, "Can't wait to hear this. You know I was teased as a child because of my hair . . . certain unpleasant boys liked calling me the little red hen while they pulled my hair. I must confess that I don't have a lot of fond memories about the fable."

"Well, this may change that. The leadership genius of the little red hen wasn't her ability to share or, if you prefer the cynical version, bribe her friends and associates. It was her ability to tie the results she wanted to the results her cohorts wanted. Connecting people to what matters most to the organization, to the team and to the other individuals involved is the hidden secret to leadership success. The little red hen understood that."

Thirty years later, after raising a family, managing a successful career and getting ready to turn around her third company, Ann had never forgotten McKnelly's words or their profound impact on her life. That summer internship had launched her very own little red hen journey with a twist. In her version of the story, she had become a master of leading results, one who worked tirelessly to convince the people she worked with to take full ownership for making the bread they wanted to make.

3

RED HEN REVOLUTION

During the next nine months, true to Ann's plan, five business units were sold, three new, strategically selected companies were acquired, Barrington's debt was paid down and refinanced at a lower interest rate, and $500 million in equity funding was raised. The company's stock price had jumped from $35 to $71 per share.

Ann walked into Rogers Barrington's office in downtown Chicago for their weekly one-on-one session. She sat down in one of the overstuffed chairs grouped around his large coffee table and next to the Rembrandt.

Rogers got up from behind his desk and joined her. As he placed his cup of coffee on the table, he asked Ann the following question: "The board and the family are very pleased with the financial improvements you've made but they're concerned about employee morale. The divestitures have added to the growing unrest and uncertainty in the workforce. The board and the family are getting antsy."

"Barrington has regained 50% of its market value in nine months. You'd expect shareholders to be delighted. What am I missing?"

"Oh, don't get me wrong. The board and the family are very pleased. They just want to know what's next."

Financially, the company's situation was turning around, but the organization's mindset and commitment relative to owning results had barely budged. Ann's focus up to now had been on completing the chores of financial turnaround and strategic repositioning, largely through her own expertise and direction. But she'd also been closely observing her direct reports, getting to know their direct reports and understanding their businesses. Now that the financial bleeding had stopped, she was ready to start focusing on the internal organization. She knew the company's strengths and weaknesses inside and out. It was time to start making bread together. It was also time for the senior leadership team to become a real team by getting aligned around the results that mattered most at Barrington going forward.

When it came to the rest of the company, the vast majority of Barrington's 30,000 employees were still on the fence regarding the divestitures, acquisitions and financial changes they were seeing. Most were reasonably engaged and genuinely cared about the company. They just didn't see any need for personal change nor what was in it for them. Out of loyalty, they usually worked hard and put in extra hours when required. However, their focus on tasks with seemingly little awareness or connection to the ultimate results the organization needed to produce made it clear they were going through the motions of well-intentioned but naïve allegiance. They were just doing what they'd always done to keep their jobs, but none of them felt they were really responsible for the company's success . . . none of them were taking the necessary risks to create greater value.

"So where is their anxiety coming from, Rogers?"

"Some of our senior leaders and a few long-time employees have complained about not being involved."

Ann wanted to ask him who had complained but she didn't because she expected the complaints even though she had thoroughly discussed each of her turnaround moves and decisions with her senior leadership team before taking action. The senior team's input had been marginal at best. Her three functional heads over finance (CFO), technology (CTO), and human resources (CHRO), who were more tactically than strategically oriented, deferred to her on everything. Her six Group Presidents, who managed the company's twenty-one strategic business units were much more focused on their business groups than on the company as a whole and their ownership of corporate decisions showed it. Consequently, Ann managed most of the corporate repositioning herself through investment and commercial bankers, deal-making lawyers and carefully selected consultants. She'd clearly been up for the challenge and actually excelled at driving the turnaround.

"I expected some members of the senior team to be critical, even though they had ample opportunity to be more involved. What about the long-time employees? What are they saying?"

"They're worried about more changes and not having any say or input."

Ann nodded. A dangerous minority of employees, some of them long-timers with over thirty years with the company, was actively and annoyingly disengaged. Approximately twenty percent of the workforce did just enough to get by and avoid being written up, while sending a lot of negative energy through the grapevine. That negativity fed a false but believable rumor mill of impending layoffs and more divestitures along with an active character assassination campaign focused on the leadership team. Their disruptive behavior and vocal cynicism would definitely slow down the company's needed change.

"Well, you can prepare the board and the family for what's coming by telling them that everything is about to change," Ann said with a hint of frustration over the board's and family's apparent lack of gratitude. Ann knew that the negativity was going to get worse before it got better and she'd attempted to prepare Rogers for it, but he was only partially aware of the employees' complete lack of ownership for achieving results and she knew it. Monday morning quarterbacking was heating up from the board and major shareholders because Ann's focus had been primarily strategic and financial to this point. Had she been the first non-family CEO, their criticism might not have been so pointed and rapid. Rogers had been holding them at bay by continually reminding them of the significance of Ann's uncanny successes with debt management, strong acquisitions and great returns on the divestitures.

"I could use some talking points, Ann. A few specifics should satisfy them."

Ann leaned forward with that now familiar look of resolve in her eyes. "You can start by telling them what we're not going to focus on first."

"Okay," Rogers said warily, because Ann never stopped surprising him. "I'm all ears."

"It's a long list, Rogers," she said, pausing a moment to let the comment sink in. "Let me make something clear, it's not that the things on this list aren't important, they are. They're just not *most* important. So, they won't be our first focus."

"Go ahead. I can take it," he said, still unsure of the *what and why* behind her thinking. He opened his notebook and took out his pen.

"I'm reading this from an alphabetical listing of today's hottest management and leadership concerns," she said as she pulled out a single sheet of paper.

Rogers' eyes grew larger. *She's obviously prepared for this.*

"We're not going to focus on accountability, alignment, best practices, coaching, communication, conflict resolution, continuous improvement, creative destruction, critical thinking, culture transformation, customer commitment, data stewardship, diversity, downsizing, emotional intelligence, employee engagement, execution, feedback, habits, innovation, leadership development, learning transformation, organizational health, psychological profiling, productivity and performance, quality management, recognition, reengineering, relationships, sales training, six sigma, speed to market, storytelling, strategic choice, talent development, team building, trust, virtual reality or workforce technology."

Rogers had stopped taking notes after the first six. He would just ask her for a copy.

When Ann finished her litany, Rogers looked like a deer in headlights. "Okay. Then what *are* we going to focus on?"

"Results!"

"I know that . . . but how? Results don't just manufacture themselves."

"Let me ask you something," Ann said while staring searchingly into Rogers' eyes. "When you think of cause and effect, do you see results as the cause or the effect?"

Rogers thought about her question for a few moments before answering. "Effect."

"The effect of what?"

He thought for another moment and then responded slowly. "Good strategy . . . solid leadership . . . healthy culture with high engagement at every level."

"Exactly," Ann exclaimed. "That's what most good business leaders think . . . because all of us have been trained and conditioned to think that way."

"Okay," Rogers said adding a bit of edge to his voice as he took a drink of coffee and waited for Ann's clarification of where she was going.

Ann held his gaze for a few moments. "It's backwards."

"What's backwards?"

"The whole cause-and-effect proposition is that good strategy, solid leadership and healthy culture are what cause the achievement of desired results."

"I'm going to need a little more explanation on this

one."

"Turn it around," she said, watching the confusion spread across his face and then to his body as he sat back in his overstuffed chair.

Rogers remained silent while, predictably, folding his arms across his chest. Body language was still such an obvious, yet often misinterpreted, form of communication.

Ann continued. "Instead of assuming that desired results are the effect of good strategy, solid leadership, healthy culture, and hard work; what if you assume that good strategy, solid leadership, healthy culture, and hard work are the effect of truly owning the desired results?"

Rogers stared out the windows at the lake, thinking about the subtlety, and possible profoundness, of reversing cause and effect.

Ann took another sheet of paper from her folder. She placed the single sheet in front of Rogers. On the sheet was a graphic with two conditional scenarios.

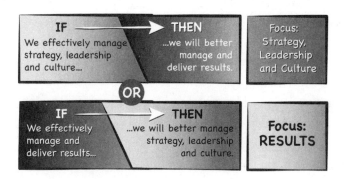

Rogers surveyed the graphic for several moments before turning his gaze toward the Rembrandt on his wall. "You're suggesting that we've been focusing on the wrong side of the cause-and-effect equation for the past several decades."

"Yes."

"How can results be a cause? I don't get it. Aren't results by definition an outcome . . . an effect?"

"When you see results as the cause instead of the effect, it compels you to reexamine how you think about, feel in relation to, and act upon the results that matter most to you, your coworkers, your boss, your organization, your customers, and your shareholders. Check with your stakeholders. Ask them what is most important. It will be results, hands down.

This requires a complete change in mindset, commitment, and behavior. It's not that strategy, leadership, and culture aren't important. They are. You can't sustain success without them. But they are not what is most important and therefore should never come first. Results matter most. How we manage and lead results has to come first."

Rogers looked down at the graphic again. "Keep going."

"I know you love college basketball. Think about the great college basketball coaches over the years, there's a wide range of styles and approaches from Mike Krzyzewski to Dean Smith to Bobby Knight to John Wooden. But they all have something in common."

Rogers nodded. "Results."

"Yes, the best coaches always put results at center stage. Irrespective of their approaches or philosophies about teamwork, personal development, character building, academics and a host of other things, their first and primary focus is on winning results. These great coaches don't let their teams get stale or distracted. They practice everyday to address results issues, results gaps, and results solutions. That's how they stay focused on the prize. Winners work every day to become winners and stay winners.

Great teams are expected to win. The best coaches have different approaches to strategy, leadership, culture, practices, habits and of course the infamous X's and O's, but results always come first. Records don't lie, results always lead to banners hanging from the ceilings, sold out stadiums, and, as you know, winning is always what makes or breaks careers. Winning results is what matters most . . . everything else flows from that. Putting results first makes their results the cause rather than the effect. But, it's also crucial to recognize that results for truly great coaches are always whole results, joint results, game of life results . . . never one-dimensional, partial or inequitable results."

Rogers confirmed his agreement.

"Most leaders and organizations approach results as an effect rather than a cause, so they focus on the means rather than on the ends. And it's led to a glut of management and leadership models that have become nothing more than surrogate religions." She paused to give Rogers time to process what she was saying. "Of course, these surrogate religions, or belief systems if you prefer, produce a lot of positive energy, but they rarely deliver the expected results or justify their cost . . . and they often compete for time and money vis a vis targeted results. Think about it, every one of the strategy-leadership-culture initiatives on this list of what we're not going to focus on has become a belief system . . . a belief system that confuses cause and effect . . . a belief system that seeks converts . . . a belief system that has become an end in and of itself . . . a belief system that distracts us from the results that matter most."

Rogers remained reflective for several moments before responding. "That's exactly what happened under the second CEO I hired. The surrogate religions thing resonates with me. I totally get it."

Ann had made a direct hit, but not by happenstance. She'd done her homework and her instincts were right.

"Why has this happened to so many business leaders and their companies? To us?" Rogers asked with genuine curiosity and heartfelt concern. He remembered, again, his second interview with Ann when she had recounted the fable of the little red hen. *She's on to something . . . something big . . . something that seems simple . . . yet something profound.*

"Whether you attribute it to complexity, disruptive change, or just getting lost in the minutia, it's slowing us down and preventing us from delivering better results. All of our systems and processes around strategy, leadership, and culture are well-meaning and provide guidelines for action planning, but they also produce disabling distractions and snowballing complexity. Sustaining the achievement of extraordinary results demands much more than we're giving. We have to work smarter and differently. I like to think of it this way—whenever people refer to their greatest victories in life, they always cite their unflinching devotion to achieving a result that really mattered to them."

Rogers looked at her with a clear sign of recognition. *He's obviously connecting the dots,* Ann thought.

"You were meant to be here, Ann. One of our board members actually described the second CEO I mentioned as always preaching a surrogate religion but never delivering what really matters. I'm now framing that experience in a much larger context thanks to you."

Ann was beaming inside, her homework had paid off. She loved being prepared, making her case and moving the needle. Rogers's buy-in was growing, which was exactly what she needed. She placed another sheet of paper in front of him to take him to the next step.

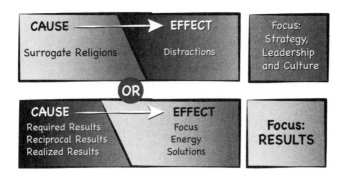

"When we introduce new strategic initiatives, leadership programs or culture change to fix poor results instead of fixing how we think, feel and act on the desired results, we're treating symptoms and not the actual sickness or disease. We're addressing the branching *effects,* not the root *cause.*" She paused a moment to let Rogers think about the new graphic in front of him.

Rogers looked at the graphic. "I get it, Ann. Tell me more about Required, Reciprocal, and Realized Results."

"We're going to completely change the way people in the company think about, feel in relation to, and act upon results by shifting their daily priorities to Required Results, Reciprocal Results, and Realized Results. Results will become our cause as never before. When we do that, you'll see a dramatic effect throughout the company. People's focus, energy, and solutions will become increasingly directed at and aligned with achieving the results that matter most—the results that create real value for customers. In other words, we'll be defining the results that are *Required* for sustainable business success, results that need to be *Reciprocal* for everyone in the organization, and results that must be *Realized* every single day, 24/7/52."

Rogers smiled at Ann's precision and thoroughness, but it was apparent that he still wanted more explanation. After all, he was the one who would have to sell Ann's approach to the board and the family. "I definitely think you're on the right track here. We've certainly experienced the pain associated with not making results our first priority. What I want to know is how the strategy gurus and leadership sages and culture high priests are going to react to this?"

"They'll accuse me of heresy," Ann said smiling.

They both laughed.

Then Ann placed another sheet of paper in front of him and allowed it to soak in. Several moments passed before she spoke again.

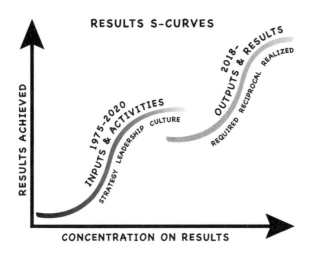

RESULTS S-CURVES

RESULTS ACHIEVED

1975-2020
INPUTS & ACTIVITIES
STRATEGY LEADERSHIP CULTURE

2018-
OUTPUTS & RESULTS
REQUIRED RECIPROCAL REALIZED

CONCENTRATION ON RESULTS

"In the end, none of the gurus, sages or high priests can argue with this reality. We have been managing and leading by inputs and activities for far too long. It's time to manage and lead by outputs and results." Ann paused, looking pensive and asking Rogers to look at the sheet of paper again. "The shift that we need to make at Barrington will be like experiencing a fundamental shift in technology—videotape to digital, cable to Wi-Fi, email to social media, data center to iCloud. It will move us to a brand new s-curve with a greatly expanded future in terms of achieving organizational, team and individual results. It's a shift we have to make, Rogers, the business demands it. Our leaders need it and the rising generations of millennials and Gen Zers will never do their best work without it."

Rogers returned to studying and thinking about the graphic at some length before looking up at Ann.

"You know I'm right, don't you?"

Rogers didn't say anything but concurred with body

language. This was the most deeply passionate and philosophical that Rogers had seen the fiery CEO. He waited for her to continue.

"I hope this doesn't come across as flippant, but I am not an itinerant preacher who's trying to gain new converts and revenue from the latest strategy processes, leadership systems or culture practices. The only thing I have to gain is better results, so I can be completely transparent and totally pragmatic. All of the surrogate religions and their burgeoning congregations won't give up until diminishing results choke them to death. That's why we need this change. Strategy, leadership and culture will always be important, just like processes, procedures, systems, policies, structure and practices will always be important, but we need to put them in their proper places . . . always after and subject to a revolutionized approach to leading results."

He enthusiastically communicated his approval. "You make a very strong case and I must say that I find myself agreeing with you. How do we implement it?"

Rogers' vote of confidence lit a fire in Ann to drive home her case with a simple metaphor. "Think of Barrington's disappointing results as an automobile with fuel efficiency problems. You can change fuels, introduce fuel additives, replace the carburetor, add a fuel-injector, replace the air filter more often, coast downhill when possible, track fuel usage at different speeds, over-inflate tires, strip the car of unnecessary components and weight, drive slower, improve maintenance, stop the engine instead of idling, get a new GPS system to better plan trips, clean the car more often and find other ways to reduce drag, turn the air conditioner off as often as possible, carpool, buy your fuel from big box retailers or other discounters, even get a fuel-saver app for your phone."

Rogers' eyebrows were raised as she finished the litany. He liked her flair for rattling things off.

"Of course, all of these things will improve fuel efficiency," Ann continued. "But their time-cost benefits are questionable. In the end, the best way to improve fuel efficiency is to replace the car with a smaller-engine vehicle, a hybrid, a turbo diesel or an electric. That's what we have to do here: change the way we approach results by getting a new vehicle. Then, we can optimize our vehicle's effectiveness and efficiency with new and better approaches to strategy, leadership and culture. The new vehicle we need is a Results Revolution."

Showing signs of uneasiness again, a slightly furrowed brow and nervous rubbing of his chin, Rogers asked, "Even though we've talked about this in general terms before, what exactly should we expect from this Results Revolution?

"This is where the little red hen comes in. The dictionary says that a revolution is nothing more or less than a dramatic change in ideas or practice. We're going to experience both."

A knowing smile changed his face. "Getting the employees' attention," Rogers said with new recognition. "And that it might be disturbing for them and me in the beginning. I do remember that part."

"Exactly," she said as she placed a final sheet of paper in front of him. "We're going to put strategy, leadership and culture in their appropriate places by forever changing how the people in this company think of, feel about and act upon results. This is the model that will guide our Results

Revolution to put results at the center of everything we think, feel and do and return Barrington to industry dominance and economic leadership."

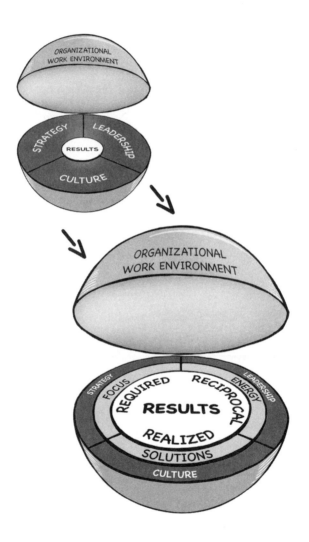

Rogers studied the model for several moments before the

smile on his face turned into a broad grin. Then, he began summarizing the model. "Effectively leading Required Results brings greater focus, which drives better strategy. Leading Reciprocal Results fuels higher energy, which develops better leadership. Leading Realized Results generates smarter solutions, which creates better culture." Rogers waited to see Ann's reaction as he was obviously anxious for her approval.

Ann began nodding and smiled brightly. "Exactly. It also works from the outside in. Better strategy facilitates greater focus on delivering Required Results. Stronger leadership drives higher energy to produce Reciprocal Results. Smarter culture fosters the creation of more valuable solutions to ensure Realized Results."

"I think I'm going to enjoy this Results Revolution . . . or should I call it the red hen revolution?"

Ann smiled. "Me too, Rogers . . . feel free to refer to the revolution either way . . . I'm sure everyone else will take liberties with the red hen version."

The meeting was over. They stood up and enthusiastically shook hands.

Rogers had made the right decision when he hired Ann Strong. He finally felt that his grandfather would be pleased. Channeling some of the old man's unusual but highly impactful charm, he said these final words to Ann as she left his office, "I'm ready for us to make the *bread* we really want to make."

"That's really what this is all about," Ann said as she turned back toward Rogers. "Getting everyone excited about enjoying that warm, savory, and delicious loaf of bread together . . . it's no more complicated than that."

Rogers ended the conversation by referencing a quote

from the late Peter Drucker: *Leadership is defined by results not attributes.* "I'm aligned with you, Ann, and I think Drucker is one guru who would be too."

"I think you're right, Rogers. Thank you for your confidence and support. Let's make this happen."

4

A SHOCKING REALITY

Ann Strong stood at the podium in front of the company's top fifty leaders. Her first year as CEO had just ended, coinciding with the company's fiscal year end of March 31st. Thankfully Barrington Corp's losses had also ended. The company recently posted its first profit in three years. Over the past ninety days, the company's stock price had jumped from below $71 to over $96 a share. The external transformation was now quite real. The internal transformation, however, was being launched today.

This was the first time in four years that the top fifty leaders had been gathered together in one room. The group was comprised of the top three levels of management—Ann, her nine direct reports and each of their direct reports. The venue was the Renaissance Ballroom at the Intercontinental

Hotel in Chicago. Despite the company's dramatic financial improvements, there was guarded anticipation in the air as the leaders awaited the words of their CEO. One leader characterized the group's collective mood as skeptically optimistic, an obvious oxymoron. Less conspicuous characterizations from other leaders were guardedly whispered around the room. The gist of those whisperings was: *the numbers are always what matter deep down at Barrington and Ann has done pretty well so far without much input from us, but will it continue? She has to get this team more engaged. If she can't, we'll just get another CEO and start over again. We're used to it.*

Regardless, the company's budding turnaround had brought this extended leadership team together once again, which was a good thing. Most of the power players in the room were expecting to hear an announcement of substantial bonuses and a new round of stock options. The room hushed as Ann Strong adjusted her microphone and prepared to speak. But no one was expecting to hear what she was about to say.

"Welcome to Barrington's first Leadership Summit in over four long years," Ann began.

A spontaneous outburst of applause erupted from the group. These leaders knew the drill. There was a long chorus of unsolicited shouts and flattering praise. Three hard years of disappointing and frustrating results had come to an end. Suddenly, celebratory excitement filled the air.

Ann waited for the clamor to die down. "However, before we celebrate too much," she said solemnly. "I need you to candidly answer a tough question for me about business unit performance. Are you open to this?"

An uneasy silence filled the room, as if a serious storm

alert had just been given. What happened next launched a journey that would change Barrington and every single person in that ballroom forever.

"Go ahead, Ann." The response came from the back of the room.

"Business unit leaders, did our operational results hit plan this year?"

The room went dead silent.

"Have we made plan in the last seven years?"

"You already know the answer to that," came the response from Jack Grossman, one of the business group presidents. There was an unmistakable twinge of irritation in his voice. His business group and one other had met their plans but the other four had not.

"Yes I do, Jack, but I want to hear it from all of you," Ann said as she stood firm in her resolve to make the point.

"No, most of us haven't," came the collective response from a majority of the group.

The mood was somber, leaders felt demoralized and the energy that was in the room five minutes earlier was now draining away.

Unaffected by the change in mood, Ann continued. "In response to this reality, I want to make a few things perfectly clear. Starting immediately, all raises, bonuses, stock options, and profit sharing in this company will require my approval, which won't be easy to get until our current culture of entitlement changes . . . and changes dramatically." She paused before continuing. "This policy will remain in place until the leaders, teams, and employees in this company learn to focus directly and continually on achieving our desired results . . . instead of completing non-essential tasks, juggling non-critical priorities, doing only what we're told, or performing non-productive work that prevents us from achieving our desired results. The choice is ours. Barrington is profitable today because of a number of financial and strategic changes executed over the past several months, but changes in operations have been minimal. So, I'm going to help each of you make the necessary personal and professional choices to drive the organizational and operational change. We will meet our results targets every single time."

Shock and insecurity rippled through the group. Their guarded anticipation and skeptical optimism was turning into resentment and dread.

For the next two hours, Ann made her case for change. Intermixed with solemn questions and intense discussions, she focused primarily on clarifying the company's four key results for the coming year. Two large screens at the front of the room displayed the following key results:

- Revenue Growth
- Profit Growth
- Results Revolution
- Market Leadership

Based on her evaluations and discussions with Rogers, the board, key shareholders, the senior team, and employees in general over the past year, Ann had concluded and obtained agreement from Rogers and the board that these were the four things that mattered most to Barrington's success and sustainability. Achieving these four key results and their associated metrics in the next year would constitute success. For Ann and her senior executive team, these deliverables were nonnegotiable. Not delivering on them was not an option, a reality she proceeded to make abundantly clear. "When I accepted this job, I began by asking myself three fundamental questions:

What are the outcomes that matter most to Barrington if we want to address current business challenges and avoid further decline?

What are the outcomes that matter most if we want to achieve major strategic and operational improvements in performance?

What are the outcomes that matter most if we want to permanently strengthen our basic business models?

"The answers to these three questions led to the identification of the four key results on the screen. You should know that Rogers Barrington and the board are in full alignment with these four key results and their associated metrics and targets. Now, I want to get all of *us* aligned."

Ann then reviewed the four key results in detail. A new slide displayed on the flanking screens.

- Revenue Growth—15%
- Profit Growth—20%
- Results Revolution—90% active involvement
- Market Leadership—1st, 2nd, 3rd or Out

The company's overall Revenue and Profitability Growth

targets for the coming year were "15 & 20"—fifteen percent revenue growth and twenty percent profit growth. The Results Revolution target was "90% active involvement"— every leader, team and employee must own the key results and tie their contribution, impact, and value add to those key results. The Market Leadership target was "1-2-3 or out"— market share for each of the company's twenty-one strategic business units had to rank among the top three competitors in their respective markets or the strategic business unit would be divested the following year.

Before lunch was served in Michael Jordan's Restaurant on the second floor of the Intercontinental, Ann told the group of fifty leaders that there would be three in-depth workshops in the coming sixty days to further immerse them in these four key results.

During the lunch of salads and crab cakes, the buzz around Ann Strong's comments exhibited a growing uneasiness. Most of the leaders were not sure how to interpret the experience, but her words were still resounding in their ears.

After lunch, each of Ann's direct reports met with their respective teams in breakout sessions to review the past year's performance and discuss key business challenges. Of course, there were lots of questions about the new policy on raises, bonuses, stock options, and profit sharing as well as the three upcoming workshops. The senior executives had no choice but to make it clear that, with the exception of knowing about the four key results, they were experiencing everything that had happened today for the first time along with the rest of the top fifty leaders. And that's exactly the way Ann wanted it.

When the leaders reconvened in the Renaissance Ballroom for a wrap-up of the Leadership Summit, Ann Strong delivered a short and sweet send off. First, she thanked them for their commitment and loyalty to Barrington and their openness to her leadership. "I also want to acknowledge that, despite our failures to hit plan in the past few years, it appears that most of our businesses are now positioned for success—a very fortunate reality."

Then she zeroed in on trust, as a business challenge. "I'm aware that I must earn your trust," she said, earnestly. Then she assumed a more playful flair, "I'm okay with that."

A ripple of nervous laughter spread through the group.

"Because that's exactly what I intend to do."

This time there was spontaneous applause, as if the group was responding with *Yes! That's exactly what you need to do.*

Ann nodded her acknowledgement of the group's retort. "As to the upcoming workshops, I have purposely not shared the details with any of you." She paused.

Suddenly, the room turned quiet and uncertain again.

Smiling broadly, she said, "But we will be heightening your interest over the next few weeks through your executive leaders."

Pockets of nervous laughter could be heard throughout the ballroom, but most of the leaders remained silent, awaiting another zinger.

"I want your anticipation and curiosities to build. These three workshops are going to change everything . . . so get yourselves ready for a Results Revolution. It's coming. And I expect nothing less from each of you than your undying effort to earn trust with me, your team, the organization, and yourselves by demonstrating an unyielding commitment to our four key results. It will work to your individual and our collective benefit."

To Ann's surprise, the group gave her an immediate standing ovation. Despite nagging anxiety for many, there was a growing admiration for Ann Strong as their CEO and leader.

Barrington Corp had, indeed, been floundering, which churned on the insides of every leader in the room to one degree or another. Ann Strong had certainly not made them happy and content, but she had both challenged them and given them hope.

They're ready, Ann thought as she visibly expressed her surprise and pleasure at the standing ovation and then returned the gesture by applauding them. *They're ready but they have no idea of what's coming. Time to make the bread . . .*

5

REVOLUTIONARIES

William W. Wright, his friends called him Will and sometimes *Triple W*, arrived in Chicago from Boston on May 1st. He was taking a yearlong sabbatical from his academic career to help Ann Strong create a Results Revolution at Barrington Corp. Will was the Paul R. Lawrence Professor of Organizational Change at the Harvard Business School and had already joined Ann in facilitating transformations at two other companies. For a tenured academic, he was unusually practical about everything, intensely passionate about helping people achieve their desired results, and gifted at making complex ideas simple and actionable. His mission at Barrington was to clarify Ann's vision of a Results Revolution and make it real for the top tier of leadership. Ann and Will had become a unique sort of episodic team. They shared a common purpose and uncanny ability to address a company's unique circumstances and issues. Theirs was no canned, cookie cutter or flavor of the month approach.

Will grew up in New England and had been teaching at the Harvard Business School for over twenty years. He was a widower. His wife of thirty years, and the love of his life, had died two years earlier of cancer. She had taught American Literature at Bentley College in Boston. He was looking forward to living in Chicago during the next year for many reasons. First, he would have a chance to re-connect with his son's family. After his wife passed, his need to see them had become even stronger. He would have an opportunity to share all the things he loved most about Chicago with them—the food and the amazing architecture. After all, his great uncle was Frank Lloyd Wright. Will's son Michael was a professor like his parents. He taught Economics at the University of Chicago. Michael was at the airport to pick his father up and take him home for a family dinner. The joyous reunion had ended too soon because Will had to find his place, get some rest, and prepare for the big job ahead. But *what a great dinner it was*, he thought. There would be more.

The next day he arrived right on time at Ann's office.

"All settled in," Ann said as she greeted him with a warm hug.

Will grinned. "You make it easy."

Ann had arranged for Will to live in a company-owned Brownstone on Astor Street in the Gold Coast historic district of downtown Chicago. "I trust everything is to your liking?"

"Historic Victorian, eclectic furniture, modern art, and a street of impressive architecture—what's not to like? Uncle

Frank is rolling over in his grave, right here in his beloved city."

Ann smiled and laughed.

"You obviously remember that I'm not a *form follows function* guy when it comes to living space. Hope you didn't have to do too much with the space."

"Don't worry about it for a second. We are just grateful to have you here for the next year," Ann expressed.

"Thank you, Ann. I'm going to feel right at home."

"That was the idea. We want you to be comfortable," Ann said, pausing. "This one is definitely going to be more difficult than the previous two."

"What's happened since we last talked?" Will asked as he sat down on the sofa in Ann's office.

"Rogers is onboard and I think he's ready," Ann said with a look of concern. "But he's been through a lot with the past three CEOs . . . and the board and family are more anxious and prone to second guessing than I expected after the financial turnaround."

"You still believe Rogers is strong enough to handle what's coming without faltering?"

Ann didn't respond immediately, which told Will what he wanted to know. When she did respond, her tone was guarded. "I expect him to crumble once or twice during the process, but I'm banking on our ability to win him back . . . as long as the senior team remains completely aligned with us."

"Is it ever any other way?" Will asked with a wry smile.

"Never," Ann replied, smiling back.

"When am I meeting with the team?"

"Tomorrow afternoon."

"Good. So, give me the full data dump on Rogers and the

senior team."

For the next two hours, Ann summarized the state of affairs at Barrington Corp. Based on their previous experience together, Ann knew exactly what Will wanted to know. How were Rogers and Ann's direct reports viewing her after one year at the helm and specifically how were they reacting to her decision to stage her focus—first, on a big financial turnaround and second, on an internal transformation? Those were the questions that Ann spent most of the two hours addressing.

In her opinion, Rogers viewed her as competent and extremely results-oriented. Her results to date certainly spoke for themselves. His reaction to the staging of her focus—something she had also done in her previous two companies with Will coming in for the transformation stage—was mixed and evolving. At times, Rogers had been confused, at other times curious, other times impressed, and still other times anxious.

The senior team—composed of a Chief Financial Officer, Chief Technology Officer, Chief Human Resources Officer and six Business Group Presidents—viewed her differently, depending on their roles. The three functional heads viewed her as fiercely independent and highly motivated, each one was surprised that she hadn't yet shaken things up inside the organization. The six group presidents viewed her as hands-off when it came to operations and a bit enigmatic, which seems to be fine with them because they'd been left alone to run their businesses. Regarding their reaction to the one-two staging of her focus, the six group presidents were in a wait-and-see mode, hoping that she would continue to be hands-off when it came to their operations.

Ann also made it clear to Will that Jack Grossman and Bob Daringer, two of the group presidents, were the strongest members of the team and the ones with the most influence on the other leaders. They would have to get on board to facilitate and secure alignment of the entire team.

"I've been sizing up these leaders for the past year. It's a solid group of leaders but they don't function as a senior team . . . they're definitely in need of a group transformation. Jack and Bob will either accelerate or slow down the process, but they won't stop it."

"Well, we both know that will be their choice, but you and I can be pretty persuasive."

"I'm counting on it . . . why do you think I went through so much trouble with the Brownstone?"

"So much for not worrying about it for a second."

There was laughter. The sort of Results Revolution that Ann and Will were planning could never happen without the senior team deciding to embrace it fully—completely of their own free will and choice.

"If Barrington's Results Revolution is as successful as the previous two, it will be time to write our book. By the way, my research on reciprocal workplaces will be completed by the end of the year. Perfect timing," Will said with added energy in his voice.

"This one has to be better, faster, and cheaper than the last two. Today's CEOs won't even consider the idea of a Results Revolution unless it can deliver a substantial return on investment within a year . . . two years max," Ann said.

"That's the beauty of this challenge. If we make Barrington work, we change the face of management and leadership forever. Your next gig will be the speaking circuit."

Ann gave Will a slightly dubious look. "Barrington first, William . . . then we can talk about a book. But the speaking circuit is your thing, not mine. My passion is leading revolutions that turn people into bread makers. If we're successful at Barrington, I'll help you write the book while I'm looking for number four."

"Revolutionaries forever."

They both loved what they did for a living.

"How are James and Sarah?" Will asked. James and Sarah were Ann's two children who lived in Chicago.

"James just got promoted to Marketing Manager at Abbott and he's been dating the same girl for more than a year."

"Nice . . . go Jamey."

"Sarah is going back to work at the law firm after eight weeks of maternity leave. She loves being a lawyer, just like her dad, but she misses being home with my two granddaughters. I think she's balancing it all much better than I did at her age."

"Sarah is amazing, so savvy and unflappable. If anybody can have it all, she can. How's the newest arrival?"

"She has red hair."

"Oh my God . . . not another one."

Ann and Will had become great friends over the past six years. They were both happy to be working together again.

"How are Michael, Mary, and little Logan?" Ann asked. "Michael's getting antsy about tenure, but I think it's in the bag. Logan just started talking nonstop . . . he's a real pistol, just like his grandma. I plan to spoil him rotten this year."

"How's their marriage?"

"She's still trying to find herself, but they're doing better. Michael's learning to temper his obsession with becoming a Nobel Prize winning economist."

"I'm so happy to hear that. They really are a lovely couple."

The two of them spent another hour catching up before Will returned to his Brownstone to prepare for his meeting the next day with Barrington's senior executive team.

After Ann climbed into the company car and greeted her driver, she sat back reflecting on the unique connection and chemistry between her and Will, wondering for a fleeting moment whether something more might come of it down the road. Right now, her focus had to remain on transforming Barrington Corp.

6

INTERPRETING EXPERIENCE

After spending his first day at Barrington discussing the company's situation with Ann, Will held his first meeting with Ann's nine C-suite direct reports: CFO, CTO, CHRO and six Business Group Presidents. Based on Ann's and Will's previous work together, they decided that Ann should not attend his first meeting with her team to give Will a head start on building his own relationship with the team.

Will began the meeting by sharing some of his background. He was the author of a dozen books and numerous articles for publications such as the *Harvard Business Review, The Wall Street Journal, The Atlantic Monthly, The Economist, Chief Executive,* and *Psychology Today.* Over the past three decades, he had provided consulting services to hundreds of CEOs and companies in a variety of industries. After a personal introduction, he told a few stories about organizational transformation and then described his and Ann's past two transformation experiences. Thirty minutes later, he opened up the meeting to questions.

The first few questions were safe, dealing with Will's background, experience, and past work with Ann. Once the group of executives felt more comfortable with him, they became less cautious. Not surprisingly, an hour into the meeting and things started to get a little gritty and very real. This team of executives was still trying to figure out its leader, Ann Strong, despite the fact that she'd been at the helm for almost a year.

Jack Grossman, one of the two Business Group Presidents that Ann had talked about the day before, asked the question Will had been waiting for.

"How does Ann expect to motivate people to change by essentially freezing compensation?" Jack said. *I can't believe it,* Jack thought to himself. *The company is struggling to get its act together and we're sitting here with another consultant.* Part of Jack's frustration came from the fact that he knew he'd been considered for the CEO spot.

Jack was the ultimate pragmatist and had never been shy about expressing his displeasure about whatever was blocking company results. He was also one of two Group Business Presidents that had actually hit plan this year. Needless to say, he was feeling a little ignored and betrayed. However, given his political acumen, he begrudgingly demonstrated respect for the company's newest CEO and her consultant by choosing his words carefully, despite the fact that he was still wound up about having to attend this meeting. The last thing this company needed was another consultant-designed boondoggle. *This team needs to hold people accountable for results, so we can win.*

Instead of answering Jack's question, Will turned back to the group. "I'm assuming the rest of you have a similar question or concern?"

There was some initial hesitation followed by head nodding all around. Jack's influence was evident.

"I'd like to hear what each of you thinks about this issue before we address the *why* behind Ann's decision to tighten her control over compensation."

For the next few minutes, Will heard a variety of comments, including: fear is not a lasting motivator, any change we get will be temporary with this approach, we're going to lose good people over this, and how does she think depriving employees from sharing in the company's success will make them want to change?

When the venting had run its course, Will said, "I'm surprised that none of you has made the connection." He let his comment sink in for several moments.

There were several frustrated, even angry, looks darting around the conference table.

When the mood in the room had reached an apex of discomfort, Will said, "Think about it . . . asking for help to reposition the corporation but not getting much other than business as usual from all of you who are understandably focusing on your own teams. Then relying on outside resources and her own efforts to turn things around. Now having baked the bread, she's not willing to share it with anyone who won't step up, own the company's needed results, and perform the work to deliver those results going forward. Anyone see it?"

The executives looked defensive, feeling manipulated and not liking it. None of them was really listening at this point, except Jack Grossman, the Business Group President whose question had initiated this deep dive.

Jack nodded his head in calm recognition. "She's acting like the little red hen. That's how she turned around her two previous companies. She comes in, more or less singlehandedly improves financial results, and then refuses to share the benefits until everyone steps up to a higher level of ownership and commitment. It's theater. Four CEOs in seven years . . . she has to do something different and dramatic to capture our attention. Mr. Wright, here, is part of the show."

Everyone in the room acknowledged Jack with a *you gotta be kidding me* head shake or sigh . . . *the little red hen, is this really happening?*

Will was part of the show and he was enjoying his role. He was also impressed with Jack and knew that he would not be easily won over. Ann's detailed description of Jack's background ran through his head. "As a Group President, Jack had impressed everyone with his performance. But impressing people was not new for Jack. Throughout his life and career, he had always been a *natural* leader. He married his high school sweetheart, Jane. The two had been homecoming King and Queen together, almost inseparable from the first moment they laid eyes on each other. In their senior year, he had set the school's passing record on the football field while she was captain of the cheerleading squad. Jack and Janey, as he had always called her, were the classic storybook couple. Jack converted his all-state football honors into a full ride to Michigan and seemed destined for greatness in college and maybe even the pros. Then he folded his knee back during his junior year at Michigan and was forced to find a new dream.

Fortunately, Jack's grades had never slipped during college. A tough competitor, according to those who knew him, he was as good academically as he was athletically. Several large corporations that sourced Michigan for talent offered him internships during both his junior and senior years. Ultimately, he chose GE as the place to start his business career.

"Thank you, Jack," Will said with a warm, appreciative smile and nod toward Jack. "Let's reexamine the folktale, because many leaders and organizations seem to have forgotten its age-old wisdom and common sense."

At this point, the emotional angst in the conference room began subsiding like air seeping from an over-inflated balloon. The group of executives was now listening, albeit circumspectly.

Will asked for their patience as he recounted the story of *The Little Red Hen*, who lived together with a dog, a cat, and a mouse. They did very little while the little red hen did all the work. Then he started to directly cite from the original folktale.

One day while gardening, the little red hen found some grains of wheat. "Who will help me plant this wheat?" she cried.

"Not I," said the dog.

"Not I," said the cat.

"Not I," said the mouse.

"Then I will," said the little red hen.

Then the little red hen planted the wheat, watering and weeding the ground each morning until the wheat began to grow. When the wheat was ready to harvest, she asked, "Who will help me cut this wheat?"

The response from each of her colleagues was again, "Not I." So, the little red hen harvested the wheat by herself.

The same thing happened when the little red hen asked for help to take the wheat to the mill to be ground into flour, to gather sticks to make a fire in the stove, to mix the flour with other bread ingredients, to knead the dough, put it into the pan, and bake it in the oven. Each time, her colleagues responded, "Not I." So, the little red hen did all of it alone.

When smells from the baking bread filled the house, the dog and the cat and the mouse came running into the kitchen.

As the little red hen took the beautiful bread out of the oven she asked, "Who will help me eat this bread?"

"I will," said the dog.

"I will," said the cat.

"I will," said the mouse.

"No, you won't," said the little red hen. "I did everything required to bake this bread and I'm going to eat it . . . all by myself." And she did.

After that, whenever there was work to be done—bread to be made—the little red hen had three very enthusiastic and energetic helpers.

When Will finished reading the folktale, he looked at Jack Grossman and said, "Ann is simply trying to lead the way . . . in a new way."

Jack nodded his agreement, but resented the suggestion that he and his peers were lazy dogs, cats, or mice. "You're right. She has acted largely on her own to make a lot of bread for Barrington during her first year as CEO. But that doesn't mean we haven't played crucial roles. Our businesses and functions are keeping this ship afloat."

"She's well aware that many of you are making great progress and, of course, she fully realizes that Barrington cannot operate without you, your teams, and the rest of the company's employees. What she wants is for everyone, not just this senior team, but everyone to be as 'all-in' as she is. She wants everyone making the bread and enjoying the benefits of bread-making along with her."

Suddenly, the air seemed to get sucked from the room.

Will waited for the negative reactions and red faces to show themselves again before continuing. He wanted to engage their emotions.

Jack Grossman and Bob Daringer, another Business Group President and a close friend of Jack's, were exhibiting a lot of oppositional and cynical body language—shared eye rolls, snickers, and a few sidebars. They were obviously annoyed. *How could a children's story apply to them?*

Will had seen this sort of response before, especially at this stage in the process. What exacerbated this situation was something Ann had shared with him. Jack and Bob had worked together several years ago at General Electric and were considered two of Barrington's best leaders. However, the results in their two groups had not been enough to offset the lack of results in the company's other business units because both of their groups were still climbing out of substantial loss positions." Will would have to stay close to them throughout this process . . . or risk losing them and their influential support. He knew they were both winners. Their business groups hit plan this year, but the fact that they both missed plan last year combined with the lackluster performance from the other business groups had diminished their achievements.

When Ann described Rogers Barrington's assessment of these two key players, Will had paid extremely close attention. At GE, Jack and Bob had been solid players, destined to run major business units. So, when Barrington poached Jack mid-career, it was viewed by many as a real coup. Then Jack convinced Bob to come, yet another coup. Jack had an uncanny ability to accurately assess his own strengths and weaknesses, quickly size up his competition's vulnerabilities, and stay open to new ideas, at least when he took the time to analyze and integrate them into his own mindset. But he could also be prickly, cynical, and brutally direct. He did not mince words. In fact, he was not afraid to express his perspective with angry expletives to make his point. He recently made his numbers, but the way he did it showed, at times, a distinct disrespect for others, which was counter to one of the company's core values. In fact, his coffee cup had a quote on it, *It's not whether you win or lose, it's whether I win that counts.* He thought that this quote demonstrated his sense of humor. Others, not so much.

Of course, Ann had analyzed Jack and Bob's winning of results over the past year more thoroughly than they realized. The truth was that Jack and Bob frequently took advantage of Barrington's other leaders by soliciting their cooperation but not giving it in return. While she admired their strengths, she was already figuring out how to address their bad habits.

Bob, was more of a maverick than Jack, always looking for new ways of doing things and often giving those around him the impression that he was a renegade and wild card. But

Bob, like Jack, always delivered results. His group of business units had brought more new products to market in the past three years than any other group. He was a virtuoso violinist in college and an entrepreneurial genius. While attending Stanford, he'd started three businesses—a violin rental business, a homemade pizza business, and a computer repair business. Bob was the consummate idea man, quick study and an extremely creative problem-solver.

As Will observed and reflected on the group, he watched Jack and Bob share another *can you believe this shit* look with each other. It was time to move on.

"Ann Strong clearly believes that results are what matter most, but she has an equally powerful belief about fairness, one of Barrington's timeless values. All of you are still gainfully employed here at Barrington because you've kept the company's businesses operating . . . although at a level that all of you have agreed requires substantial improvement. Does anyone disagree with that assessment of the state of the company?"

All of them wanted to argue with Will, but, as is always the case in business, senior leaders know that *the numbers are the numbers.* For that reason and that reason alone, no one disagreed. Will knew this would be the case based on his conversations with Ann. She had confidence in this team; they just needed to become uncompromisingly focused on delivering the key results.

"This brings us to the heart of the matter. The story of the little red hen symbolizes, in a simple yet elegant way, what we have to do individually and together to WIN. Ann wants to make lots of bread with each of you and your teams . . . sharing it generously with all of you . . . in fact, sharing it with every single employee in the entire company. And I mean really sharing it . . . unlike any success sharing you have ever experienced. That's where she wants to go. But it will take everyone owning and delivering the necessary results for that to happen. That's why the tightened compensation policy applies to everyone . . . even you." Will paused.

The mood in the conference room was still slightly defiant.

"She's serious about creating a Results Revolution at Barrington . . . but she can't do it without each of you. Of course, there will be plenty of bread for those who help make it happen."

This was met by another prolonged silence, just as Will expected. Anything else would have concerned him. True to form, the silence was symbolic of the senior executive team's reluctant acknowledgement, grudging acceptance, and pragmatic concern for what was to come.

Will adjourned the meeting with a homework assignment. "Take some time over the next couple of weeks to think about a few questions:

What should a Results Revolution look like in terms of changing how people think, feel and act?

How should a Results Revolution address processes, systems, and structure?

Why would you, your direct reports or anyone else in the company willingly embrace a Results Revolution?

What is it about the 'bread' itself that will cause you and the people on your teams to jump out of bed in the morning enthusiastically committed and completely intentional about making bread together?

"I want you to get specific and personal about what it will take for each of you to feel like jumping out of bed every morning to come to work."

The senior leadership team's first meeting with Will Wright was now over but they would meet again many times over the coming months. The next time they were scheduled to meet as a group was in three weeks for the first of three daylong workshops along with their direct reports. It would be the second time in two months that the company's top fifty leaders were getting together. Historically, change efforts at Barrington had focused on everyone else but the top leaders. This was clearly different. Change was definitely afoot at Barrington.

As the senior leaders left the room, Will informed them that he would be available for consultation prior to their next meeting. Three of the executives set up times to get together, two others said they would call him after checking their schedules. Jack Grossman and Bob Daringer said nothing. The remaining two, the CFO and CHRO, stayed afterwards to talk process and next steps.

One more step toward Barrington's Results Revolution had been taken. Now the challenge was to prepare for the first of three workshops that would set the stage for changing everything at Barrington.

Later that evening when Jack Grossman arrived home, he unloaded his frustrations on his wife, Janey.

"You won't believe what we've got going on at

Barrington," he said as he walked to the liquor cabinet. "I need a drink."

"What now?"

"Our new CEO thinks she's the little red hen and she's hired a Harvard Business School professor to teach us the fairytale's underlying wisdom . . . so we can use it to create a Results Revolution," Jack declared before downing a double shot of Pappy Van Winkle's Family Reserve, 24-year aged bourbon. The really good stuff.

"You've gotta be kidding."

"I wish I were," Jack said as he poured himself a second double.

"She actually thinks of herself as the little red hen?"

"Apparently."

"Oh, my God! What woman in today's society wants to be referred to as a *hen?* I'm sorry, sweetheart . . . fairytales at work?" she said as she gave her husband a heartfelt hug and kiss on the cheek.

"It may be time for us to purchase that dream villa in Tuscany."

7

STAGE ONE
PREPARATIONS

Rogers, Ann, and Will sat around the large coffee table in Rogers' office, drinking their morning coffee and getting ready for a discussion about tomorrow's first offsite workshop.

"Is the team ready for tomorrow?" Rogers asked as he looked at Ann and then at Will.

"Yes, Rogers. They're more than ready," Ann said, confidently. "I think most of them are wondering why it's taken me so long to focus on them. Others are hoping I never will."

The three of them laughed.

"They'll find out tomorrow, won't they?" Rogers said, smiling at Ann and then looking at Will.

"After meeting with the senior leadership team and then spending time with each of them individually," Will injected, "it's clear they have a lot of misgivings and questions about what's coming, but that's pretty natural at this point. From my point of view, they're anxious and ready for a transformation . . . but wary given their experience over the past few years."

Rogers nodded at Will. He liked Will and respected his knowledge and experience when it came to corporate transformation. But it was the rapport and harmony between Will and Ann that made him most comfortable. They had forged a partnership ready to revolutionize his company.

"Needless to say, they're a little uneasy about the red hen revolution thing," Ann said.

"Do they know about the new compensation policy?"

"Only the senior team," Ann said. "I asked them to not share it with their direct reports prior to tomorrow's session, but I'm sure some of them have shared it with their key players and confidants."

"I'd love to be there tomorrow to see this first hand, but I know it's better if I'm not there. This is about you and your team, Ann."

"We'll give you a blow-by-blow debrief when it's over," Ann said to reassure Rodgers.

Suddenly, Rogers' face turned serious. "Who are the pivotal detractors and supporters on your team?"

Ann and Will looked at each other before Ann responded. "As you can imagine, Will and I have discussed this question at some length in the past few days. Jack

Grossman and Bob Daringer are the pivotal players . . . on both extremes."

"What do you mean?" Rogers asked.

"Right now, they're our biggest skeptics. And detractors. They've been stirring the pot since Will's meeting with them. However, they also have the potential to become our biggest supporters and allies. The team respects what they've done in their business groups during the past two years. And, let's face it, they are the two most likely internal candidates to succeed me as CEO. I've been watching them closely over the past year. Either one of them could be a future CEO of Barrington, and since Bob is a few years younger than Jack, both of them could potentially take a turn."

Rogers looked back and forth between Ann and Will. "Hiring Jack was one of the best things your predecessor did, Ann. Jack has made us relevant again in the Consumer Electronics Industry. We're not dominating the industry yet, but we're a strong contender in a few niches. And, of course, Jack was responsible for bringing Bob onboard. Bob is now making us relevant in the Industrial Automation Industry. Two great hires for Barrington." Rogers paused. "So how are we going to turn these two rising stars into our allies?"

"It starts tomorrow morning," Ann said. "We have to get Jack and Bob fully engaged in the process, no matter what it takes. Our expectation is that they will be vocal from the beginning, which will help. If they're not sufficiently vocal, Will and I will give them the necessary nudge."

Rogers nodded enthusiastically. "Good."

What Ann knew about Will was that his name was a perfect match for his strength and guts. She called him 'iron' Will and he wasn't just good at this work, he was world class.

He'd helped transform more than a hundred major corporations in the past twenty years. What Will knew about Ann was that she was on her way to becoming one of the top CEOs in the game. What they both knew was they had to get Jack and Bob to join them willingly in this revolution . . . to get the rest of the team to come along in the process.

Will would have to manage Jack and Bob as a sub plot while focusing on the entire team of fifty leaders. But he knew in his gut that this was a winnable contest. He also understood that there were never any guarantees. It would be challenging, contentious, and unpredictable. A Results Revolution was a living, breathing experiment and the leaders involved had to really want it—it could not be phoned in. It was a demanding process of peeling the onion one dialogue at a time.

"Will, why don't you take Rogers through an overview of tomorrow's agenda."

"Tomorrow is about building greater focus on what matters most," Will began. "The challenge we face is that when business results are not acceptable, senior leaders often turn their attention to strategy. However, preoccupation with business strategy can create distraction and disengagement in the organization, diminishing the delivery of what matters most. The only solution is to strengthen the company's focus on getting the results that matter most. We do that by developing clear and concise Required Results for the enterprise, each of its teams, and every position in the organization. We start with the top fifty leaders. Everything in the workshop is designed to increase clarity and reduce distraction around the results that matter most. Relative to Jack and Bob, they are all about results. They were trained at

GE. They'll see the focus on Required Results as common business sense. When they do, we'll take advantage of it. They are both outstanding business executives, they will get this, and when they do, they'll embrace it. I asked them to be vocal from the beginning of our session tomorrow and to not hold anything back. I think I'll be dancing with them early on in tomorrow's session."

Rogers was smiling at what Will had said. He also knew that Jack and Bob would not need any encouragement to speak up. He was pleased that Ann and Will thought about Jack and Bob the same way he did.

Will handed Rogers a sheet of paper with a graphic on it. "This is the shift we need to begin tomorrow."

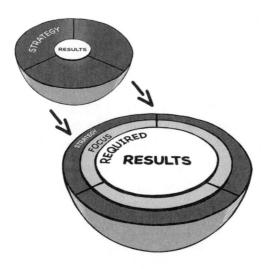

As Rogers examined the graphic, Will continued. "I know Ann has already discussed this model with you. Tomorrow, we'll be focusing on the first third of the model. Required Results are designed to be the first lever for change, facilitating focus on what matters most and reducing the distractions associated with strategy preoccupation. Establishing clear Required Results is the key to successful strategy execution."

"So, this is what the first step toward a Results Revolution looks like?"

"Exactly," Ann said. "Tomorrow we begin transforming the way these leaders think, feel, and act relative to what matters most at Barrington."

"Revenue growth of 15%, profit growth of 20%, a Results Revolution with 90% active involvement, and market leadership that means 1-2-3 or we divest," Rogers said, pleased with himself as the goals rolled off his tongue with ease.

"Perfect. That's how I'll kick things off tomorrow morning," Ann said. "Morning Joe with extreme focus."

The three of them smiled.

"Make it happen, Ann. I have full confidence in you . . . in both of you."

"Thanks, Rogers. We won't let you down. The red hen revolution goes into full-scale execution tomorrow."

Their meeting adjourned with smiles all around along with feelings of unity, resolve, and anticipation . . . but Ann and Will knew those feelings wouldn't last.

8

MORNING JOE
WITH FOCUS

The first workshop was on May 16th, in the Avenues
Ballroom at the Peninsula Hotel in downtown Chicago. Ann
kicked off the session with a review of the company's
Required Results for the current year—Revenue Growth,
15%; Profit Growth, 20%; Results Revolution, 90% active
involvement; and Market Leadership, 1-2-3 or out. Once
again, she made a compelling case for why the Required
Results were crucial to the company's short-term and long-
term success.

"As we discussed in our leadership conference a
month ago, the achievement of these four results are required
to deliver what matters most to Barrington Corp this year.

Their achievement will be evidence that we are on the path to realizing our vision of (1) becoming one of the most admired companies in America, (2) creating superior value for our customers, and (3) ensuring a great place to work for our employees. You'll hear me refer to them as Required Results because they are required to demonstrate that we are succeeding and building for our future. In a nutshell, these four Required Results are:

Strategically critical, meaning that they are tied to our vision, mission and key business challenges—creating real customer value, producing superior products and services, and sustaining a great place to work where people can be successful.

Individually meaningful, which means everyone in the organization can understand and connect to them on a personal level every single day. Everything we do should be related to achieving Revenue Growth, Profit Growth, a Results Revolution, and Market Leadership.

Operationally measureable, meaning that we can measure our progress toward these Required Results on a daily, weekly, and monthly basis. If we don't measure our progress, we won't make progress.

"Some of you may be thinking that the required result of creating a Results Revolution will be hard to measure. That's one of the things we're going to discuss today. So, let's dig in. By the end of the day, we want to be able to tie everything we think, feel, and do at work to these four key results. That's what Required Results are all about—what matters most to the business must guide what matters most for each team and each position. Today is about connecting the dots. You'll be introduced to a simple SPEC for Required Results. It's the same template I used with Rogers and the board to develop the four Required Results for Barrington as a whole. SPEC is an acronym. **S** is for Sales . . . Revenue Growth. **P** is for Profit . . . Profit Growth. **E** is for Employee Engagement . . . Results Revolution. **C** is for Customer Satisfaction . . . Market Leadership. I want everyone in this room to start connecting what they do every day to these four Required Results by developing their own sub-SPEC for Required Results for every team and position in the company. In other words, how do each of you and your team of direct reports and their teams of direct reports contribute to, impact and add value to Revenue Growth (S), Profit Growth (P), Results Revolution (E) and Market Leadership (C)."

When Ann finished her opening remarks, she briefly introduced Will Wright. As Will joined Ann at the front of the room, she said, "Will is going to be our facilitator during these next three sessions and our ongoing coach as we implement a Results Revolution here at Barrington. Our work together with him won't be effective without candor, so get to know him . . . and don't hold anything back."

Will expressed appreciation for Ann's confidence and then immediately asked a provocative question, "Do all of you understand that Ann is expecting us to launch a Results Revolution during our time together today?"

Jack Grossman, the Business Group President who two weeks earlier had made the connection between Ann and the little red hen, quickly responded. "Will, we don't know you yet, and you really don't know us, so please don't be offended by what I'm about to say—"

Will acknowledged Jack's posturing without being offended. He expected it and was ready. "We're going to get to know each other very well over these next three sessions, and in between, so go ahead, say what's on your mind. Let's get the ball rolling and see where it takes us."

"Do you know how many times we've heard about getting better results during the past few years? I've only been here two years, but I've heard all the stories. Our people are tired of change that hasn't produced real results."

Will responded calmly and a bit playfully, "I'm assuming it's a lot."

"You're damn right," Jack snapped back.

Despite his flaws of being prickly, cynical and, at times, prone to yelling, Jack had the power to energize people through his transparent style and direct approach. Most people seemed to be engaged by his charisma and some were not. But it was always better to counsel with Jack rather than to confront him. He was a force of nature and his focus was always on the bottom line, which made him hard to argue with and relatively easy to follow.

"Let me ask you a question, Jack. Have you taken part in any personal change in the past two years that has impacted the company's results in a meaningful way?"

"We've made more changes in my business group during the past two years than any of us thought possible . . . so I assume that you understand why we're tired of hearing about it . . . make sense?"

Will had hit a nerve but he wasn't done yet. "I hear you . . . but you didn't answer my question."

"I'm telling you the unvarnished truth here. What question am I not answering?"

Everyone was riveted by the theatre playing out in front of them, but no one was quite sure of what they were actually witnessing. Some of the leaders were leaning forward in their seats, others were cringing a bit, and still others were looking around to see reactions.

One leader muttered, "Jack's crazy. He's going to bury himself."

Another responded, "No way! Jack's fireproof."

A third remarked, "Whatever this is, it's fun to watch."

Will seemed unaffected by the building emotion in the room. He repeated his original question again, "Have you experienced any personal change in the past two years that impacted company results in a meaningful way?"

Jack's energy level jumped as he became defensive, "What do you mean by the words *personal* and *meaningful*?"

"Individual changes in how you work or lead that have led to significant improvements in company results." Will's body language was inviting and expressive. He was a genuine person. Most people were disarmed by that and believed he truly valued them, which he did.

Jack seemed taken aback for a moment. He looked like a boxer who'd just taken a right cross to the jaw. "Not really . . . I don't like how that sounds . . . but that's the truth." He recovered quickly with an answer that caused some eye rolling from others in the room. "I guess you could say I've been in execution mode, not development mode. We learned some powerful practices at GE."

Will opened the question to the other leaders in the group. "What do the rest of you think about this? Have any of you experienced personal changes during the past few years that have led to significant improvements in company results?"

"Jack's right—we've been focusing on the basics with steady progress, but the holes we're digging out of are making it slow going," Bob Daringer said, trying to both support his friend and get Will to back off this line of questioning.

Bob and Jack's talents were complementary, they had clicked from the time they first met and continued to do so every time since. Jack was like a dog digging for his favorite bone when it came to problem resolution. He could always get to the core of things and knew how to identify the truly high leverage opportunities. Bob would then seize upon the root cause as a welcome challenge and come up with not just inside the box solutions but multiple flavors of outside the box solutions as well. Jack had actually felt compelled, at times, to ask Bob to back off on the ideas because he needed time to think them all through. They were a good team and often heard to say, *we always have each other's backs.*

But Will was undeterred, "Why has it been slow going?"

"We know we haven't been able to turn things around from the inside," Bob said. "Ann knows it. That's why you're here. The problem is we've seen a lot of new faces with a lot of great sounding ideas over the past few years. Why should we believe you are any different than the others who have passed through the revolving door?"

"You shouldn't," Will answered as if the dialogue had been scripted, but his disarming style put everyone at ease. "However, this time the change is going to come through you, not someone from the outside. That's the difference."

The room went silent and stayed that way for several seconds. *This is different from the previous three CEOs. Ann is different. This consultant is different and he's not talking consultant-speak.*

Will continued. "Our first exercise this morning is intended to deepen this dialogue about personal change and creating a Results Revolution. Are we up for it?"

"We're more than ready for something that actually works, Will," Jack said, less defensively this time. What Will was saying and how he was saying it was starting to make him curious.

Ann winked at Will from the back of the room and then stepped to the front. She asked everyone to get into cross-functional, cross-business groups of three for an exercise she called *Winning*. It was a game designed to simulate the common struggle of getting people aligned across multiple teams and levels. It begins with defining what *Winning* really means for individuals, teams, and the entire organization.

Will and Ann had agreed that this group of leaders needed a powerful common experience to launch the requisite mental and emotional transformation required to turn this company around. When the leaders had settled into their sixteen separate trios, Will began, "All of us understand the importance and benefits of winning and being part of a winning team . . . its common sense, right? The issue is turning common sense into common practice. So, why do so many organizations fail to identify and define what *Winning* looks like for every individual and group in the organization?"

The leaders slowly began to answer his question.

One leader responded, "People need to understand the

goal and then take responsibility to make their contribution to it. We don't have time to handhold anyone here."

Another said, "People get lost in the whirlwind. So, they lose touch with what winning means and looks like."

Yet another injected, "People like to hide in activity. They naturally move to what they know best and like. They don't really want to take ownership for outcomes or winning."

Will seemed satisfied with the responses. He nodded his approval before continuing, "Would it be safe to assume that, as leaders, you are familiar with wading into uncharted waters with only a fraction of the information needed to take action?"

"Yes," was the collective and resoundingly confident response.

One leader added, "With all due respect, if we're not, we shouldn't be here."

Another said, "We know our business. Most of us have been doing this for a long time."

"So, given your management roles and competitive drive, if I give you the barest minimum of instructions and a one-page scoring sheet, is it safe to say that you'll figure out the game and eventually achieve success?" Will looked around the entire room for confirmation.

The group of leaders gave him exactly what he expected, reactions of pride and over confidence.

Ann smiled from the back of the room, she knew what was coming.

"The experience we're about to have together exposes how competitive drive and simply being human can make achieving desired results extremely difficult. So, listen

carefully to my instructions. You'll only hear them once."
Will paused. "The objective of this game is to score as many
points as you can."

He began handing out the scoring sheets. "As you can
see on the scoring sheet, there are multiple approaches to
scoring points—working together, performing independently,
or a hybrid of the two. You will have the opportunity to
choose which approach to apply in each round. You and your
team of three are solely accountable for determining how you
choose to score points. There will be ten rounds of decision
making and scoring. Record your points after each round. I
will announce the opening and closing of each round. Talking
to other trios within your larger group is not allowed, except
when I call for a discussion period. No trio will be confused
as to how points are scored after the first round. You and
your trio will determine how you want to proceed. Once
again, your objective is to score as many points as you can.
From this point on, even if you ask, neither Ann nor I will be
providing you with any further instructions until the ten
rounds are over."

The leaders were chomping at the bit to go. The game
moved quickly into high gear. Confusion over the
instructions, the objective, and the scoring was apparent, but
the participants were off and running, determined to figure it
out so they could win the game. This was typical for action-
oriented executives who were familiar with leading in what's
often described as *the absence of all known facts*.

After completing the first three rounds, the groups were
given a discussion period to speak to each other. The energy
level surged as everyone focused on the rules of the game,
strategies to score, making promises regarding how to

proceed, and their own trio's scores. Their comments ranged from "this game is life" to "your approach depends on whose ox is being gored" to "what's the purpose of this exercise, how do we win?" to "nobody's doing what they say they will do and I hate this" to "it's about the need to work as a team, align our approach, honor our commitments, and make sure we don't surprise anyone."

After several more rounds of competitive play and posturing, the groups of three were given a final discussion period to apply everything they had learned in an effort to maximize their points. What arose from the final rounds in all but a few groups were mostly groans of frustration and disappointment. The common learning seemed to be that it was much harder to win in organizations than anyone in the room had imagined at the start.

"We should have asked a lot more questions before we jumped in. No wonder organizations struggle with this," remarked one leader.

Other leaders were shaking their heads in disbelief and looking to Will for an explanation of what had happened. But he was not about to let them off the hook for their own collective and individual learnings.

"So, *you* tell me what happened?" Will asked.

After a moment of silence, there was a flood of overlapping responses. The energy in the room was intense and unbridled. Clearly, every leader in the room had been visibly affected by the experience.

Jack Grossman commented that the game had elicited more emotion from this group of leaders than he had seen in any prior company meeting. "Some people are still fuming. In fact, I have concerns about the safety of a few of the last-minute spoilers."

There was nervous laughter in the air.

Others turned their frustration toward Will, criticizing him for being unclear and vague about the rules from start to finish. In contrast, others quickly came to Will's defense saying, "You can't blame Will for your decisions. He said we needed to figure it out. Everybody made their own bed."

Will stepped to the front of the room and began more actively guiding the dialogue. He started by asking whether all of the groups fully understood the rules of the game by the third round.

Most of the leaders begrudgingly admitted to understanding the rules well before the third round. Then they all began glancing at each other, exchanging obvious looks of embarrassment and vulnerability. The room went quiet again, as though some of the initial indignation had been replaced with contrition.

Will used the opportunity to pull the leaders forward even harder, "If you understood the rules of the game and were aligned around what to do, why was it so hard to win?"

There was a long pause as Will's probing question lingered in the air. The rationale for *Winning* had been clear, but the group decisions, actions and communications were all over the map. Will knew many reasons why. In most cases, winning the game had shifted from a rational decision-making process to an emotional getting-even process because clarity and partnership were missing. To illustrate this reality, Will pivoted the line of questioning, asking the leaders to explain the patterns of their choices.

Breaking the silence, one group admitted to making non-team and unproductive decisions out of frustration and revenge. All three of them offered comments. They said, "It was about being irritated with the approach of some trios and then disagreeing about playing the game to win at the expense of others. We agreed to work together, but not everybody did what they said they would do. We got burned when we tried to work together, so we started working independently and not communicating our real intentions."

The obvious question was *why?*

Will took advantage of the moment to bring the dialogue to a crescendo. He asked the group to consider how often results are derailed in similar ways in real life.

One leader said, "Apparently it's impossible to deliver on multi-team or multi-level goals unless the overall expected results are clear from the beginning."

Another said, "Objectives must be repeatedly communicated, collectively shared, thoroughly discussed, individually owned, and actively reinforced."

"Overall results must be easy to understand at all levels," chimed in another.

"We can't expect our employees to be engaged and committed to achieving the desired results if we can't demonstrate that same behavior ourselves," came from another leader.

Finally, one leader summed it up this way: "This exercise highlights just how difficult it is to get everyone to understand the big picture and willingly commit to winning together. This seems particularly true if there is a chance to achieve more personal gain by concentrating more on your own individual or team results."

Will loved what he was hearing. But it was still too early to expect them to operationalize their learnings. He segued into the rest of the day's agenda by asking another simple question, "When leaders and organizations experience disappointing results, what do they most often focus on to fix things?"

Answers ranged across the board, but, not surprisingly, most of them fell into one of three categories: improving strategy, strengthening leadership, and changing culture. *It's always that way,* Will reflected, *our business schools have definitely made an impact, time to change that impact.*

Will displayed a graphic on the two large screens at the front of the room. "Do these three improvement categories—strategy, leadership, and culture—capture most of what you talked about?"

Whenever results are unacceptable, we usually turn our attention to improving Strategy, Leadership or Culture. But focusing on Strategy, Leadership and Culture often amplifies distractions and disengagement, which diminishes results.

Heads nodded and a few leaders called out, "Yes." Then, the ballroom went silent as the fifty leaders read and mulled the words in the box below the graphic.

"Most organizations and leaders typically focus on rethinking or repositioning strategy, developing or replacing leadership, and changing or shifting culture to improve results," Will said. "The problem is, focusing only or myopically on strategy, leadership, and culture doesn't cut it... at least not in terms of causing and sustaining long-term results. Here's the brutal reality of teams and organizations: the more they focus on strategy, leadership, and culture, the less they focus on the needed results." He paused. "As you can see in the graphic, too much emphasis on strategy, leadership, and culture can actually diminish rather than increase results."

Will's comments were met with looks of disbelief.

Smiling to himself and relishing the moment, Will continued. "Leaders in today's organizations often focus on the wrong things first. It's our natural tendency to attempt treating the symptoms before addressing the underlying ailment."

More silence and surprise, but the looks of disbelief were shifting to curiosity.

"What leaders, teams, and organizations need to focus on first and foremost are the results themselves—Required, Reciprocal, and Realized Results. The only reason strategy, leadership and culture exist is to enable and facilitate the delivery of targeted results. Results are what we're going to concentrate on for the rest of the day."

Will clicked to a new slide that presented the central model of the workshop. This would become their guide for creating and sustaining a Results Revolution at Barrington.

"It's time to introduce three powerful levers for change to keep all of us focused on what matters most: Barrington's four Required Results."

A few heads were nodding at the simple elegance of what Will was presenting, but most of the leaders in the room were awaiting more enlightenment.

This is the perfect break point for lunch, Will thought to himself. It was almost noon.

The leaders were definitely engaged, but they needed a break to process what they'd experienced.

"We're going to address each of these three powerful levers for change—Required Results, Reciprocal Results, and Realized Results—one at a time. We'll dig into Required

Results when we return from lunch."

"I have a question before we go to lunch," piped up one of the leaders.

Will nodded, "Go ahead."

"Are you saying that strategy, leadership, and culture get too much focus or that they're too disconnected from the desired results?"

"Both," Will said, letting the answer sink in. "Great question. My answer and the evidence behind it will become painfully clear this afternoon."

There was laughter throughout as the group of leaders broke for a buffet lunch at the back of the ballroom. Laughter was crucial for Will. His facilitation style intentionally courted and fueled it based on reading the groups' facial expressions, body language, and tone of voice when commenting or asking questions. He knew from experience that this group of fifty leaders would not be able to make it through this process without plenty of laughter.

9

OVERCOMING DISTRACTIONS

After lunch, the leaders were divided into cross-functional, cross-business groups of five people each. Ann and her nine direct reports were distributed across the groups, one per group. Their assignment was to thoroughly discuss the whys behind the four Required Results that Ann had unveiled last month and reiterated again this morning.

- Revenue Growth—15%
- Profit Growth—20%
- Results Revolution—90% active involvement
- Market Leadership—1st, 2nd, 3rd or Out

"Open, direct, and candid communication is absolutely essential for this discussion to have any value. All questions, concerns, issues, and obstacles are fair game. Don't leave anything unspoken or unaddressed," Will said. He waited a moment before continuing. "An effective strategy is crucial to any business. We rely on it to help define and clarify our Required Results, but strategy is the rudder, not the boat. The only way the boat arrives at its destination is through effective execution. In other words, the strategy has to deliver the results it was created to deliver or it becomes ineffective, valueless and distracting."

He then put a graphic on the screens at the front of the room to illustrate his point.

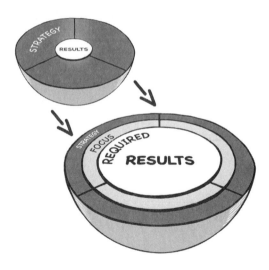

"As you can see in the graphic, we prevent undue preoccupation with strategy by applying one of the levers for change. We call it Required Results. The real value of this lever for change lies in its *distraction-busting focus* on what matters most to the organization. Any questions or comments?"

One person asked, "Why do companies get so distracted by strategy?"

"Because they're always looking for a more perfect strategy. But the plethora of different strategies to choose from can be overwhelming. A mediocre strategy well executed is always better than a brilliant strategy poorly executed. It's a knowing-doing gap. Our knowledge doesn't do us any good unless we apply it. Delivering the Required Results provides the only true evidence that an organization is effectively executing on its strategy. By the way, that doesn't mean you should be content with a mediocre strategy or stop work on developing a better strategy. It means always making sure your current business strategy is aligned to deliver your Required Results."

Another leader asked a follow-up question, "Can you explain exactly how this lever of change you call 'Required Results' solves the problem?"

"Successful strategy execution is only demonstrated through the achievement of Required Results. The single most important aspect of strategy execution is to turn it into Required Results. Great strategies fail whenever the Required Results are not delivered."

There were no other questions, even when Will remained silent for several more seconds, so he prepared them for the discussion they were about to have in their cross-functional, cross-business breakout groups of five leaders each. He would find out soon enough if they were still confused.

"Before we begin discussing the whys behind Barrington's four Required Results, I want you to send someone from your group to get one of the flip charts along the far wall and bring it back to your group."

Each group responded quickly, sending one of their ranks to fetch a flip chart and easel.

When the commotion died down, Will continued. "I'd like you to take fifteen minutes to discuss how Barrington's business strategy and its various business unit strategies are linked to, related to, or directly associated with the four Required Results. Use the flip chart to capture all of the connections. Key words are all you need to record. Fill at least one page. You've got fifteen minutes."

After fifteen minutes of robust discussion and writing on flip charts, Will had a spokesperson from each group summarize his or her group's experience. In every case, the connections between strategy and the four Required Results were abundant. When Will asked the entire group to capture the primary takeaway from this exercise, he was surprised by the CFO's articulate response.

The usually quiet James Grand, who had been Barrington's Chief Financial Officer for only three years and had never seen the company make a profit until now, said it beautifully. "Seems that the key takeaway is pretty clear and simple. While strategy can be complex and intricate and endlessly adaptive to market forces, it must always clearly translate to specific outcomes that make the business viable. Strategy has to be developed and executed to deliver Required Results. Strategy is the servant of results, not the other way around."

"Exactly."

There was a hush of recognition in the room.

"Now I'd like you to take another fifteen minutes to dig deeper into the whys behind Barrington's four Required Results. At the end of fifteen minutes, each breakout group will present a two-minute summary of its discussion. Your summary should focus on why these four Required Results matter most to Barrington Corp today and how you expect to overcome the challenges the company will face in achieving them. Begin. Raise your hand if you have questions or would like additional input."

More robust discussion filled the Avenues Ballroom for the next fifteen minutes followed by a wide variety of insightful and inspiring two-minute summaries. The final stage of this exercise was to make a compelling case for change. Will asked each breakout group to combine with one other group, moving from ten to five groups.

"Your assignment for the next twenty minutes is to write a compelling case for change. There's only one way to make the case for change convincing . . . and that's to answer the Whys . . . all of them . . . until they're collectively understood. Who remembers the three questions that Ann asked herself when she began developing the company's four Required Results?"

Jack Grossman quickly raised his hand, "What outcomes matter most to avoid decline, produce real improvement and strengthen our business models?"

Will was impressed. "Exactly. Thank you, Jack. You *were* listening," Will said playfully.

"I was and still am."

The room broke into laughter.

Will smiled broadly at Jack and the rest of the group.

"To determine what matters most, we always start with the big Whys.

- Why do these four Required Results matter most?
- Why do we need to face the challenges associated with achieving these four Required Results?
- Why should we take ownership of these four Required Results?
- Why are these four Required Results so critical for this year?

Then go to the other whys your people might ask. Once you've sufficiently vetted all of the 'Whys,' build your compelling case for change around the most captivating and energizing whys. Your compelling case for change can take any form you like—paragraph, bullet points, logic sequence, cause and effect, cost-benefit summary, etc.—but it cannot exceed three hundred words in length," Will said with a grin.

There was a round of moans and groans throughout the room.

"Be ready to present your compelling cases for change in twenty minutes. If you need more time, there won't be any."

Another round of laughter filled the ballroom.

"Of course, there will be a prize for the most compelling case."

This time there were hoots and hollers as the five groups went to work.

Exactly twenty minutes later, the five groups came back with very compelling cases for change, but one of them was hands-down the popular favorite. It crackled with energy, connecting like a lightning bolt in people's minds, partially because it was the shortest at fewer than 125 words. Their prize was a bottle of *Robert Craig* Cabernet for each member of the group. Here was their truly compelling case:

Revenue Growth of 15%
Profit Growth of 20%

- If we don't grow at 15 and 20, we won't have bonuses, stock options, promotions, new products and services, satisfied customers, engaged employees, happy shareholders, or future opportunities.
- If we do grow at 15 and 20, we will have plenty.

Results Revolution, 90% active involvement

- Join the Results Revolution or lose control, autonomy, opportunity, and money. We must learn how to deliver the desired results, year in and year out.
- Now, you get to choose—90% in to win.

Market Leadership, 1-2-3 or Out

- If we don't lead our markets, we'll become also-rans.
- If we do lead our markets, we'll become magnets of talent, customers, investors, suppliers, vendors, acquisitions, investment, deals, media, and more.

After debriefing the exercise, Will sent the leaders to break. Then, he walked over to Jack Grossman and Bob Daringer, who were chatting with a few of their direct reports in the corner. Their demeanors had definitely changed. Most of the skepticism he'd seen earlier was now gone, but not all of it.

Placing his hands on their shoulders, Will excused himself for interrupting and guided them away from the others. "I sense that both of you are still wondering about the takeaway value of these sessions. I want you to know that I respect that. In fact, I view your scrutiny of the value add as one of the main reasons why your business groups are outperforming the others. So, here's what I'd like to ask of you both: please reflect on how your business groups achieved their results and how they could be even better. Suspend any preconceived notions or judgment until after the first two sessions. At that point, if you don't see real, tangible value in this process, we'll stop it and adjust appropriately."

Jack and Bob looked at each other before Jack spoke for the both of them. "I'll be honest with you, Will; both of us were at a 'two' on a scale of 'one to ten' when you and Ann started this process." Jack looked over at Bob before continuing, "Right now, we're probably at a six. This morning has been valuable and the energy in the room is impressive."

Bob nodded his head in agreement. "We're usually on the same page."

"Good. If both of you aren't at an "eight, nine, or ten" by the end of our next session, we'll stop the process," Will returned.

"I never give 10's," Bob said, "but it's a deal..."

"Perfect," Will added.

Once the leaders had returned from their fifteen-minute break, Will transitioned into the next segment: What Matters Most for Each Team. He asked each of Ann's direct reports to move into breakout groups with their own direct reports. There were nine complete teams in the room. Since Ann's team was with their teams, Ann would roam. Their assignment was to develop Required Results for each of their teams—Required Results that would contribute to, add value to, or otherwise impact and influence achievement of the company's four Required Results.

Thirty minutes later, they came back together into one group to debrief. The ensuing discussion was forceful and revealing for everyone as each team presented their four Required Results.

Jack Grossman, President of the Consumer Electronics Business Group, presented his team's four Required Results. Jack's direct reports, each one a strategic business unit head, committed to contribute greater revenue and profitability growth than some of the other business groups because their businesses—home automation devices, vehicle electronics and GPS, health and fitness wearables, personal drone markets, and virtual reality—were experiencing such high growth rates. Their revenue and profitability growth targets were 30% and 20% and would be achieved through a variety of new product introductions. Market leadership of 1, 2, or 3 would be accomplished by divesting their printer components company and acquiring two innovative companies in the health and fitness wearables and personal drone markets. A Results Revolution would be accomplished by rolling out these workshops throughout the entire business group with 100% active involvement from its leaders.

When Jack finished presenting his team's Required Results, he made this observation: "The focus and commitment exhibited by my team during the past thirty minutes points to the power of clarifying what matters most. Will, I'm now at a seven on this process and moving higher. You can thank my team for that."

There was an outbreak of applause.

Will acknowledged Jack's movement and his team's leadership before hearing from the other team leaders, who followed Jack's example and tone.

Ann praised the teams for stepping up. "If you hit the targets you've set this afternoon, Barrington will exceed its Required Results."

Loud applause lasted for several seconds.

Will sent them to their final break of the day.

For the third segment of the afternoon, Will paired everyone up to coach each other on identifying what mattered most to each of their respective teams. Each leader in the room was a member of at least two teams—that is, the team they were a member of and the team they led.

After everyone was paired up, Will reminded them of Ann's three questions. "Here's what your conversations and coaching should look like. Start with a variation on Ann's three questions:

- What are the outcomes that matter most if I want to make sure that my team does not fail to sufficiently contribute to, impact, and add value to the company's four Required Results?

- What are the outcomes that matter most if I want my position and my team to produce a major increase in our contribution, and value add to the company's four Required Results?
- What are the outcomes that matter most if I want my position and my team to substantially strengthen the organization's competitive advantages?

"If you have any questions, raise your hand."

After a lively exchange that continued for twenty minutes, they moved back into the nine teams, each one led by one of Ann's direct reports. Within teams, each leader had the opportunity to present his or her Required Results and receive feedback from team members.

Trish Nesbit, head of the industrial software business unit and one of Bob Daringer's direct reports, presented her team's Required Results as:

- Revenue Growth of 25% by gaining market share in the industrial project management market with their new AutoPM product,

- Profit Growth of 35% by significantly increasing gross margin on AutoPM sales,

- Results Revolution by ensuring that every employee in the industrial software business unit is able to connect the dots between what they do everyday and the Required Results, and

- Market Leadership 1, 2, or 3 by displacing the current market leader in project management automation.

She admitted, "This isn't going to be easy, but now we can clearly see the pathway. My team is going to love this."

Bob Daringer praised Trish when she finished. "Trish is one of the most no-nonsense, strategically savvy software engineers I have ever met. So, when she says her team is going to love this, you know we've moved to a whole new level."

Spontaneous applause filled the ballroom.

As several other leaders shared their position's (team's) Required Results, it became clear that tying position Required Results to team(s) Required Results and then to company Required Results was more challenging and stretching than anyone expected. However, the process was thought provoking and motivating. Energy levels continued to climb through the end of the day. Clarifying and connecting the dots relative to the company's four Required Results had substantially improved over the past several hours. And every person in the room knew it.

Will concluded the day's session by having everyone record their Required Results—four company results, four team results (for each of Ann's direct reports), and four position results (for each of the senior team's direct reports)—on a Results Map card from their workbooks. He used Trish Nesbit's results map as an example by taking a picture of it and displaying it on the screens at the front of the ballroom.

RESULTS MAP — Trish Nesbit

Required Results	Organization Barrington	Team Industrial Automation	Position Industrial Software
Revenue Growth	15%	20%	25%
Profit Growth	20%	25%	35%
Market Leadership	1-2-3 or Out	Stay at 3	Move from 2 to 1 AutoPM
Results Revolution	100% Victory or nothing	100% Rollout to entire team	100% Daily focus on results

When everyone had completed their results maps, Will turned the floor back to Ann for a final wrap-up.

Ann reminded the leaders that this was the first of three sessions. Session two would be held in two weeks to address making results reciprocal. The homework assignment she gave to every leader in the room was to meet with his or her direct supervisor during the next fourteen days to review and confirm their Results Maps—a summary of the Organization, Team, and Position Required Results. She also asked them to discuss the whys behind their Results Maps.

There were a few questions, which she and Will answered quickly and concisely. Both of them knew that the Results Maps would provoke robust and focused conversations over the next two weeks.

Ann had always been a student of great leaders and organizations in the world and throughout history. She was a voracious reader with intense intellectual curiosity. So, it was no surprise that she concluded the session with a story about Warren Buffett and Berkshire Hathaway.

"Berkshire Hathaway's performance has been nothing short of amazing over the years. The company's secret? Everyone knows what matters most: beating the S&P index by investing in the right businesses and trusting talented management with operating decisions.

"The company's investment and acquisition criteria are simple:

> *Large purchases (at least $75 million of pre-tax earnings unless the business will fit into one of our existing units),*
>
> *Demonstrated consistent earning power (future projections are of no interest to us, nor are 'turnaround' situations),*
>
> *Businesses earning good returns on equity while employing little or no debt,*
>
> *Management in place (we can't supply it),*
>
> *Simple businesses (if there's lots of technology, we won't understand it),*
>
> *An offering price (we don't want to waste our time or that of the seller by talking, even preliminarily, about a transaction when price is unknown).*

"What matters most is made perfectly clear by Warren Buffett to Berkshire Hathaway's operating managers, acquisition candidates, and shareholders. We want the same to be true of The Barrington Corporation. The only way we're going to accomplish that is by making our Results Maps so vital in guiding what we do on a daily basis that strategy, strategic initiatives, strategic adjustments, and everything else that goes on in our businesses don't distract us from what matters most."

When the meeting adjourned just after 4:30 p.m., Jack Grossman came up to Will. "Bob and I are now both at an eight . . . and actually looking forward to the next session. You'll also be happy to know that all of our preconceived notions and judgments have been completely suspended. Nice work, today."

Will thanked him for the feedback and set up a time to meet with them both during the next week. He would be spending plenty of time coaching each of Ann's direct reports in the next two weeks. *That's how it works . . . because leaders and organizations never spend enough time focusing on what matters most.*

10

AFTER SESSION DRINKS

Jack and Bob met for drinks at Untitled, a trendy whiskey lounge a few blocks from the Peninsula Hotel. They had both met with their direct reports for a few minutes after the session to get their reactions and feedback.

Jack arrived first and was sitting at the bar in the Whiskey Lounge thinking about the day. When Bob arrived a few minutes later, Jack was sipping an Old Fashioned.

"Sorry I'm late," Bob said. "My team wouldn't stop raving about today's session. You surprised by that?"

"Hell, yes," Jack responded. "Janey's never going to believe that I'm buying into this little red hen stuff."

They both laughed as Bob ordered a Manhattan.

"I'm in the same place," Bob said. "Amy could not believe it when I told her about Ann Strong, the little red hen story, and the freeze on compensation. So, what are you thinking? Today's session obviously had a big impact on both of us."

Jack took another sip of his drink while contemplating his response to Bob's question. He'd been asking himself the same question for the past hour. "What surprised me most about today was the excitement and engagement of my team. You and I talk about results incessantly, but something connected with them today at a different level."

"Yeah. It's both encouraging and discouraging."

"Exactly."

"What was it that struck a chord in everyone today? I'll be honest. It affected me, too."

"Two things are rolling around in my mind," Jack said. "First, Ann has done a great job of making Barrington's four Required Results crystal clear, and she's established her credibility with the financial turnaround. The leaders in that room today respect her and Will. Second, I think that chaotic, confusing game we played this morning actually captured the group's attention. My team couldn't stop talking about it. It's as if they finally admitted to themselves and each other how manipulative, political, and self-serving people can be in organizations. Some of them even confessed to me that they had, at times, outright blocked certain peers from achieving their goals. They did it because they were pissed off by the sabotage they perceived from others. The truly amazing thing was that they also began to talk openly about accidentally acting win-lose at times because they didn't always see or understand the bigger picture. I think it woke them up—actually opened them up."

"Totally agree. People want to win. Most of them don't want to cheat, but sometimes they make mistakes. It's not always an issue of ethics. It's usually about emotion and not betrayal or revenge. I think the day-long focus on results had a huge impact on my team. Trish kept saying, 'We've never taken the time to get this clear about what matters most to the company, the business group, and our teams.' Frankly, it was a little embarrassing. I'm like you. Both of us talk about results relentlessly. Maybe that's the issue—we're the ones doing all of the talking. Today, they did the talking."

Jack nodded. "They also had the opportunity to make choices about their own contribution, impact, and value add to what matters most."

"What do you think about Ann's decision to let Will do most of the heavy lifting today?"

"She can be a little too hands-off for me, but I'm not complaining," Jack returned. "She's leaving us alone to build our businesses—Warren Buffet style. That's a model that works. I think she's very clever."

"Meaning?"

"Just like the little red hen, she's already proven her bread-making capability. Now she's waiting for everyone to join her. Will allows her to play her role. He's the messenger. I certainly didn't like it a couple of weeks ago, but I'm warming up to it. His opening questions this morning were unsettling but brilliant. I've been thinking about how I need to change personally all damn day."

Bob laughed as he took a drink. "They're both brilliant," Bob said. "She said nothing about the little red hen today, and neither did Will. But they both know that every leader in that room has heard the story of her as the little red hen and they expected to get hammered with it."

Jack acknowledged her shrewdness and then snickered as he sipped at his drink. "She's the star of the show. And you're right. It was brilliant not to say anything about the little red hen today. We'll hear about it in the next session on reciprocity . . . which will be perfect timing."

"How much do you know about the next session?"

"Will referred to it as a pivotal session because it deals with making results reciprocal. He called the lack of reciprocity in today's organizations the single biggest blunder of modern leadership."

"Interesting. I know you liked Will's questions this morning, but do you like him?"

"He's good . . . not too academic . . . results driven . . . a little dogmatic as times, but I like him. He lends credibility to what she's doing. They make a good team."

"I like him, too. They play well off each other."

"Rogers may have finally found the right CEO for Barrington, even if it wasn't me."

"Let's drink to that. Your time will come," Bob said as he raised his glass.

"Cheers. Yours too. Let's hope we feel the same way after the next session."

"I actually hope we will. Ann and Will seem right for where we are. Even though we both met plan last year, we need to keep improving our results—we owe it to both of them, the company, and ourselves."

"I am too buzzed and tired right now to productively think any more about it, but I agree we should embrace what they're doing. Who knows, we may even improve ourselves?"

Bob winked and chuckled, acknowledging Jack's lingering preoccupation with personal change. *Jack needs this and he knows it. Perfect.*

Jack smiled. "I'll take care of this. Say 'hi' to Amy."

"Same to Janey. See you in the morning."

As Jack paid the bill and left the underground lounge, he found himself reflecting on the simplicity and power of what Ann was doing.

11

PIVOT POINT

Rogers walked into Ann's office at Barrington's corporate headquarters in the Chicago suburbs. She and Will were waiting to brief Rogers on tomorrow's second offsite workshop as well as give him a progress update.

"I like being at headquarters again. The atmosphere has already changed. Employees greet me and look me in the eye again."

"As it should be," Ann said. "Things are definitely changing, Rogers. Can I get you anything? Water, coffee, tea?"

"Water would be great. I'm down to one cup of coffee a day and my body is thanking me for it."

"Smart man," Will said. "I'm not too far behind you at no more than two cups a day."

The three of them sat down in the sitting area in Ann's office.

"I talked with Jack and Bob the other night after our Bridge Communities fundraiser. They were very positive about the impact of your first workshop and seemed genuinely excited about tomorrow's session."

"We've been working closely with them and their teams since the first workshop. Like we discussed the last time we met, they are key influencers on the senior team. Their support for the results that matter most to Barrington, plus their modeling of a Results Revolution mindset, are crucial to our success."

"They're modeling it," Rogers said with a smile. "They both pulled out cards and showed me the targeted results for their business groups and each of their direct reports."

"Good to hear. We'll build on that tomorrow," Ann said, returning Rogers' smile. "We focused on Required Results in the first workshop. Tomorrow, we'll focus on Reciprocal Results. It will be challenging for many of them because it's not something they've done before."

"Reciprocity. The more I've thought about it since our first discussion of the little red hen, the more I realize how afraid we are to talk about it in organizations. It's a huge blind spot."

Ann nodded at Rogers without saying a word, pleased by his new awareness.

"Think you'll have any resistance from Jack and Bob?" Rogers asked. Then, he answered his own question. "Seems like they should be naturally attuned to this."

"Both of them practice it with their direct reports, but they do it informally . . . and they certainly don't refer to it as reciprocity," Ann returned.

The three of them acknowledged the reality.

"For Jack and Bob, tomorrow will be a formalizing . . . and operationalizing . . . of what they're already informally doing. We'll help them get clearer and better at it tomorrow. Tomorrow, we need to create a pivotal shift in how these leaders think, feel, and act relative to making results reciprocal. It will be a major shift for most of them."

Rogers sat back in his chair, surveying Ann and Will. The look on his face was sober.

"Will, why don't you give Rogers a brief overview of tomorrow."

"This is the shift we'll be working on tomorrow," Will said as he placed a sheet of paper in front of Rogers.

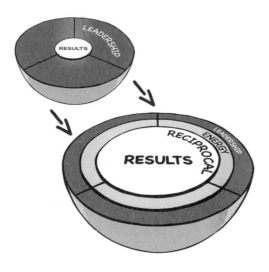

"Making results reciprocal is a lever for change that aligns leadership with the needed results. Reciprocal Results actually heighten energy around what matters most while reducing the distractions associated with leadership preoccupation around methods and development."

Rogers nodded as he looked at the graphic in front of him. Of course, he'd seen the graphic before, but isolating leadership, energy, and Reciprocal Results made him realize, even more, how important reciprocity is to successful leadership.

Will continued, "When business results are not acceptable, senior leaders turn their attention to leadership training methods, development, and recruitment. However, preoccupation with leadership can create distraction and disengagement that diminishes the delivery of what matters most."

"Just as strategy can be a distraction."

"Right," Will said. "Leadership should always be about heightening the energy around what matters most—not diminishing it. The most powerful way to heighten that energy is to ensure that the Required Results are made reciprocal for every individual on every team."

"When you think about it, that's the true essence of leadership," Ann added. "When the organization wins in the way it wants to win, everyone involved in making it happen should win in the ways that they want to win. That's true reciprocity."

"I understand why you consider this workshop to be pivotal. These leaders are going to be afraid that if they introduce the idea of Reciprocal Results to their people, it will be like opening Pandora's box to a host of miseries and evils—unreasonable expectations about advancement, demands for higher compensation, and heightened dissatisfaction."

"That's the challenge, Rogers," Will said. "Our ace in the hole is that Reciprocal Results are tied to Required Results—you can't get one without the other. All of them know it . . . even though most of them may be unconsciously suppressing, ignoring, or avoiding it."

"Why? Because we know we can't satisfy everyone's desires?"

"Yes, because making results reciprocal is hard. It requires us to understand each other at a deeper level. It also requires creative thinking and innovative solutions that we don't think we can muster or deliver. All of this leads to the perception that we'll be creating another *time waster*. It's not about scarce resources. It's about scarce motivation. Of course, understanding to make it work will help drive motivation. In tomorrow's session, we're going to help them see the collective and individual benefit of unleashing everyone's untapped energy through Reciprocal Results. We'll also simultaneously reengage them on the business of the business—Required Results."

The smile on Rogers' face grew larger now. "You have me more excited about the impact of this workshop than the last one. This one should cement the last one."

"Yes, and it only gets better with the third one, Rogers," Ann said.

"I believe that, Ann. Thank you for what you're doing for this company . . . both of you. Good luck tomorrow. I'll be anxious to hear about it and see the impact."

The meeting ended with firm handshakes and warm embraces.

Rogers' comfort level with Ann at the helm of Barrington Corp was definitely rising, but the disruptive nature of what she was doing had not escaped him. Rogers had always been a pragmatist, but his last three CEO mistakes made him more skeptical than he'd ever been. *Ann has made this work twice before, but twice is hardly a proven path. The fact remains that if this starts going south, I'll pull the plug on the little red hen faster than you can say 'reciprocity,' regardless of what Wall Street might say about it. If we're going to fail, we're going to fail fast and course correct again.*

The thought sickened him.

12

OATMEAL
FOR ENERGY

Ann kicked off the session. "There is no greater binding force in teams or organizations than the Required Results they must deliver to survive and thrive. Required Results draw us together in a common cause. People work hard for money . . . they work harder for great leaders . . . but they work hardest for a common purpose they are truly committed to. Today, we are going to learn how to take greater advantage of this primal binding force. In all honesty, getting alignment around specific results is in and of itself a revolution for most organizations. Leading effectively starts and ends with defining, clarifying, and achieving results at the organization, team, and individual levels. Research shows that 85 percent of organizations fail to clearly define, effectively communicate, and rigorously monitor progress toward Required Results."

There was heightened curiosity in the ballroom as everyone pondered her words.

Ann allowed the silence to linger before asking her direct reports to present their Results Maps.

For the next forty-five minutes, each member of the senior leadership team took four to six minutes in front of the group to show his or her Results Map on the two large screens and discuss contribution, impact, and value add for the current fiscal year ending March 31st. Of course, all of the Required Results had been thoroughly vetted, revised, and approved during the past two weeks prior to this session.

By all accounts, the experience was riveting as every one of Ann's direct reports showed how they expected to connect the dots between their teams' Required Results and Barrington's Required Results. One leader described the experience as 'inspiring.' Another called it 'amazingly focused.' A third referred to it as 'long overdue.'

After that, each of the senior team's direct reports took three minutes each to present their Results Maps. Needless to say, all of them had also been vetting and prepping for the past two weeks. Every presentation was tight, clear, and energizing. In fact, the already high energy level continued to climb right up to the first break, along with an unmistakable rise in ownership.

Just what we need, Will thought to himself as he sent the group on a fifteen-minute break. When the leaders returned,

Will set up the rest of the day by displaying the central model on the screens up front.

"Reciprocal Results will drive our conversation for the rest of the day."

Will was not expecting what happened next. One of CFO James Grand's direct reports, a straightforward emerging leader at Barrington by the name of Meg Starr, said, "I don't mean to rain on this parade, because the last session was very helpful, but do we really need two more sessions on results? I think we got the message in the first session."

Will took a moment to make sure he didn't overreact. "What is the message you think this group took away from the first session?"

Meg's response was immediate and concise. "Barrington has a set of results we must deliver if the company wants to endure. All of us need to utilize those results to formulate supporting results within our respective teams to ensure we're all aligned in delivering what matters most to the company."

"So, you think that will be enough to get us where we want to go?"

"It is for me. I'm ready to help Ann make bread."

Laughter and applause filled the ballroom.

Smiling at Will, Ann gave him the nod to go ahead.

Will knew where he needed to go with his response but it was going to take some time. Meg was a millennial, a Wharton MBA graduate with honors, and a key part of the future of Barrington Corp. If he could convince her of the importance of two more sessions on results, he could convince anyone. "How many of you share Meg's point of view?"

More than a dozen hands went up.

As Will surveyed the raised hands, he immediately realized that most of them were Millennials or Gen Zers. "I'd like to hear from some of the rest of you."

"We agree with Meg," said Seth Daniels, another one of Barrington's emerging leaders. "The results ownership message has taken hold. We get it. In fact, I think most of us have a lot of passion around it. Some of us are wondering whether we need to spend another two days deepening our commitment when we're already there. You and Ann have done your jobs . . . and done them well."

"Meg and Seth have captured it. We're ready to make this happen. We get the *what,* now we need to better understand *how* and *why . . . the whole why.*"

Three more leaders expressed agreement with Meg and Seth, using similar language.

"Have you discussed this as a group?"

"We have," Meg said.

"How many of you in the room, regardless of whether you participated in these discussions, feel similarly to what has been expressed?"

Twenty-one hands went up.

Will moved aside as Ann walked from the back of the room, her eyebrows raised and demeanor serious. "I'd like you to stick with this for the next two hours. If you do, I think you'll find the *why* and the *how* becoming much clearer. However, anyone who wants to continue this conversation at lunch is welcome to join me," Ann said in a solemn tone. "After lunch, if you're still questioning the value of what we're doing here, you don't have to stay . . . and I promise, there will be no judgment or consequences for leaving. I sincerely appreciate your candor and transparency this morning. Keep it up."

The room was silent and motionless.

"Will, let's continue," Ann said.

Will moved back to the front of the room. "Making results reciprocal means becoming transparent about what matters most to you, personally and professionally. It also means knowing what matters most to your boss, personally and professionally. And, it means understanding what matters most to your team members, personally and professionally."

The fifty leaders seemed a little taken aback by Will's call for transparency around personal results. Of course, most of them had been involved in detailed, sometimes difficult, personal discussions when negotiating their own employment contracts and those of their direct reports. But, none of them had ever been asked by any leader in any organization to share what mattered most to them, personally and professionally, as a formal part of the business planning process . . . or results dialogue.

While fully expecting to see surprised looks on the leaders' faces, especially after the mini-revolt against further discussion about results, Will smiled to himself because he knew the next phase of growth was about to break through. *Assuming I can keep them in the room.*

Will quickly moved to the next exercise by asking the leaders to think of three or four people in the group who knew them well and would not hesitate to talk candidly or push back when necessary. Then, he asked everyone to pair-up with one of those three or four people.

Twenty minutes earlier, the group had been electrically alive and fully on board with the learning process. Now, all of that had changed. The leaders were now more pensive. When everyone was paired-up, they listened circumspectly to Will's further instructions. "Your purpose in this next round of discussions is to identify the things that you most want to obtain and accomplish, personally and professionally, while working for The Barrington Corporation in the next year. In other words, Reciprocal Results are what motivate your effort to deliver the contribution, impact, and value add you presented this morning."

The faces looking back at him suggested that they heard his words but didn't necessarily comprehend them. The 'personal and professional' combination seemed to be throwing them. Despite his simple instructions, Will realized that the assignment would take a few moments to sink in. Before he unleashed them, he introduced another acronym.

"Let me give you another template similar to the one Ann gave you for Required Results—**RACE** for Reciprocal

Results. **R** is for Rewards and Recognition. **A** is for Autonomy and Freedom. **C** is for Common Purpose and Challenge. **E** is for Expansion and Growth. Use the template to guide your discussions. The important thing is to make these Reciprocal Results your own . . . what really matters to you, personally and professionally. I'm going to give you forty-five minutes for this exercise. Allow each other a few minutes of individual time and then share your thoughts with each other. Needless to say, this may feel a little awkward and uncomfortable for many of you, so don't be afraid to coach and counsel each other."

As Will walked around the room, listening to the pairs, he periodically rephrased his instructions and answered questions in an effort to manage the group's obvious discomfort. This was clearly not something that most of the leaders were used to doing. Their questions ranged from *how personal are we supposed to get?* to *what time period are we talking about?* to *do you want specific targets?*

Will's responses to these three questions were quick. "Very personal—what matters most," and "the next year or two," and "the more specific the target, the better."

When he walked past Jack Grossman and his paired partner for the exercise, Jack said, "You pull this off by keeping everybody in the room this afternoon and I'll be at a ten."

Will smiled at him. "You're the one who's going to pull this off . . . I'm just here to help you."

"We'll see."

They both laughed as Jack turned back to his partner.

Thirty minutes into the exercise, after most pairs had written down at least something about their personal and professional Reciprocal Results and participated in some level of mutual coaching, Will made it clear, "For results to become truly reciprocal for the individual and the organization, both have to be achieved. Achieving just organizational, team, and position results is not enough. Nor is solely achieving personal and professional results enough. All of them must be achieved."

The looks on the leaders' faces ranged from disbelief to confusion to excitement. One of the leaders with a look of disbelief blurted, "You gotta be kidding." It must have come out louder than he expected because his face turned beet red when everyone around him started laughing.

"I am absolutely not kidding," Will said.

The room went quiet.

"The latest research, including my own, on workplace reciprocity confirms that reciprocity-rich environments experience productivity levels three to ten times higher than non-reciprocity-rich environments," Will said.

This group of leaders wasn't used to seeing the scholarly side of Will Wright. Their anticipation for what he would say next was apparent.

"Neither Ann nor I want you to embrace the idea of Reciprocal Results based solely on research. We want you to embrace the idea because it makes sense to you . . . because it feels right to you . . . because you realize that we can make much more bread when we share the work and the benefits."

Heads began nodding as more looks shifted from disbelief and confusion to tentative openness and excitement. It was the best movement in energy and engagement he could hope for at this point in the process.

Ann returned to the front of the room. "If an

employee at any level in this organization is going to be fully motivated to deliver on what matters most to the organization, the team, and his or her individual position, then achieving these Required Results has to be tied to what matters *most* to that employee. That's why what we're doing today is so vital."

For another fifteen minutes, the leaders continued to coach each other on making results reciprocal. However, what should have been an exciting opportunity to explore what mattered most, personally and professionally, turned out to be a challenging, clumsy, and uncomfortable experience for most of the leaders.

"Let's put this exercise in context," Will said as he began his debrief. "When we played the *Winning* game in our last session, you seemed to leave the experience with a better understanding of the value of being clear on the Required Results. Agreed?"

"Absolutely," chimed one leader. "That's why some of us may not be here after lunch."

Laughter filled the room.

Smiling and nodding his head, Will said, "Fair enough. Ann made it clear that you can choose whether or not to return after lunch. So, before we lose some of you . . ."

More laughter.

". . . let's talk about something else that happened in our first session while you were playing the *Winning* game."

The mood turned somber again.

"It has to do with how trust comes from acting, thinking, and feeling win-win," Will said.

Some of the leaders began repositioning themselves in their seats, as if to prepare for what was coming next. No one, it seemed, wanted to miss this. And, of course, as long as Will was talking, he was keeping them from having to dive into another awkward, uncomfortable exercise.

Will continued, "All of us have expectations, regardless of whether or not we openly acknowledge or actively address them . . . as do the people who report to us. If our expectations are not met or exceeded, we get frustrated and angry, which blocks trust, honesty, clarity and win-win results. These unstated expectations must surface, if we want to maximize our success."

The silence was weighty. Will was taking them to a deeper level of understanding now, and they felt it.

"Do you remember the conclusion you came to after playing the *Winning* game?" Will asked and then paused. "What was the root cause of any dysfunctional behavior in your group of three?"

The leaders stared at each other until one of the more dysfunctional players in the game spoke up. "It was just a game . . ."

A whispering buzz began to stir throughout the group.

". . . I think you're trying to make too much out of a simple game," the leader concluded, defensiveness dripping from every word. He was one of the leaders that Jack and Bob had become concerned about during the game.

Will remained completely calm. "Is this what the rest of you believe?"

One of Ann's direct reports, Stephanie Masters, a soft-spoken influential leader who headed up one of the business unit groups, weighed in next. "Will, we hope you don't take this personally, but some of us have talked about this in depth. Our conclusion is that if the game, which was very eye opening, had actually been real work . . . well, we think people would have behaved a bit differently."

"Okay. How do you think the outcome would have been different?" Will returned.

"We think people would have been less prone to be emotional and dysfunctional. They would have taken a more compliant and collaborative approach." Stephanie began to look around the room to ensure that she had the group's support.

Will surveyed the leaders. She did seem to have their support. He smiled and then positioned himself for a difficult dialogue. "That's a fair observation," he said slowly.

The group breathed a collective sigh of relief.

But then Will challenged them. "So why do you think people behave so differently in a game? What's in it for them to do so?"

Stephanie responded, "We're not saying that people don't express emotion or frustration at work. We just don't generally operate like that when we're working together— things are generally handled more calmly because everyone understands that we can't have an unproductive free-for-all."

Will intensified his tone. "This is a question for the entire room. Are you suggesting that the kind of behavior we saw during the game does not happen at work?"

There was a long and thick pause that was followed by a tentative response from one of Stephanie's direct reports. "We don't think so," she said.

"Any other thoughts or feelings?" Will stood firm in his resolve to push the group deeper into self-awareness and honest vulnerability.

One of Jack Grossman's direct reports spoke up. "I

don't believe the outbursts we saw in the game happen as publically in real life . . . but they do happen, privately or politically."

Another leader blurted out, "Or in the informal meetings that happen after the formal meetings."

Bingo, Will thought.

More dead silence accompanied the ring of truth that now infused the room. After several seconds, a lively conversation began. There were several comments about how internal, unspoken reactions may ultimately be more detrimental to results than external, disruptive reactions. The discussion meandered for another ten minutes, eventually centering on the idea of partnership and how true partnerships foster win-win actions. Several leaders recounted their historical experiences with successful partnerships, collaboration, and win-win results.

Ultimately, a singular question emerged from the group: "How do we pull off *Winning,* and actually achieve the Required Results we were so passionate about this morning, while minimizing dysfunctional behavior, public and private?"

Barrington's top fifty leaders were now positioned to better comprehend and embrace Reciprocal Results. *One-step at a time,* Will mused.

"We're going to answer that question in the next exercise," Will said. He then asked everyone in the group to find a new partner to begin discussing their top four personal-professional Reciprocal Results with each other. He suggested that they use the four categories defined in their workbooks as **RACE** for Reciprocal Results—**R** for Rewards and Recognition, **A** for Autonomy and Freedom, **C** for Common Purpose and Challenge, and **E** for Expansion and

Growth—to guide their introspection and collaborative coaching. "Use the four categories to make sure your partner has carefully considered his or her four Reciprocal Results."

As Will observed their conversations, they seemed purposeful and probing. Identifying and discussing what mattered most to each of them in terms of personal and professional Reciprocal Results brought its own energy . . . it always did. Required Results brought focus and clarity, but Reciprocal Results brought energy and commitment.

Thirty minutes later, Will asked the group to comment on their experiences. One leader's observation seemed to capture the group's sentiment: "Oh, my God. This was one of the hardest things I've ever been asked to do, and sharing it with others only made it harder. But it felt really good . . . liberating."

Then another leader, one of Bob Daringer's direct reports, made the comment that everyone would be thinking about during lunch. "To be honest, doing this with my direct reports is not going to be easy. Human motivation is complicated and messy. In my experience, when you ask people what matters most to them, they clam up and wonder why you're asking or they think in terms of what they should want instead of what they really want. And then there's the reality that what matters most is a moving target for most people, so organizations can't really accommodate their desires. Besides, we're not in business to do that anyway—right?"

Most of the leaders in the ballroom were nodding their heads in agreement while waiting attentively for Will's response.

Will let the silence linger in the air before he answered.

"Thank you for that comment and question. That's exactly where we'll pick up after lunch . . . for those of you who decide to return."

The ballroom erupted in laughter as they broke for lunch.

This is when the real fun begins, Will thought to himself.

13

DIRECTING LEADERSHIP

Feelings of uncertainty and discomfort among the leaders lingered over Caesar salads and grilled chicken. Will and Ann took the opportunity to dive deeper with Jack and Bob and a small group of other leaders, including Meg Starr and Seth Daniels, who had questioned the need for additional sessions on results. The topic of discussion over lunch was the principle of reciprocity—why it was so crucial to success and how it was often difficult to apply inside an organization, even for the best leaders.

The two seasoned group presidents agreed on the difficulty but also acknowledged the enormous power that stems from connecting the dots between what matters most organizationally and what matters most personally.

"In one way or another, senior leaders are always doing this with their teams. Trying to figure out how to attract, retain, and motivate key players," Bob said matter-of-factly. "What you're asking us to do in this workshop is to formalize the practice . . . turning it into standard operating procedure . . . common practice."

Jack looked at Ann and then at Will. "Both of you have done a great job of clarifying the common sense of this, and that's huge because common sense is seldom as obvious to everyone as we think it is. Like I said earlier, you pull this off in terms of changing the way these leaders think about, feel about, and act on Reciprocal Results and I'll be at a ten. What do you think, Meg?"

"I'm here to listen and learn from you," she said looking at Jack and Bob. "Hopefully, by the time we finish with lunch, I'll have both the reasoning and motivation to stay for the afternoon."

The other Millennials and Gen Zers at the table seemed to agree.

"Ditto that," Seth voiced, the rest nodded.

Will and Ann expressed appreciation for the honesty and feedback before asking a few follow-up questions of Bob and Jack. They were the key to convincing Meg and Seth and the other leaders at the table to stay for the afternoon. Fortunately, both of them said they were at an eight on the overall process and expected to go higher. Of course, Bob would never admit to being at a ten, but he might reach nine and a half.

Ann was pleased, yet concerned, with where Jack, Bob, and Barrington's top fifty leaders were at this point in the process. For Will, this was the most rewarding part of what he did for a living. Whether in the classroom at Harvard or with a group of corporate leaders, he derived great personal and professional joy from watching people wrestle with the relatively simple yet wonderfully profound idea of Reciprocal Results. Tapping into the power that comes from truly tying together what matters most organizationally and personally was what had ultimately solidified Will's working relationship with Ann Strong.

Initially, Ann had been inspired by Will Wright's ability to translate complex ideas, but that was only one facet of her explanation for their ongoing Results Partnership. During the past few years, she had developed a much deeper understanding and appreciation for this truly unusual teacher. Will was a smart, practical, and personable consultant, who seemed to instinctively understand how to get at the underlying needs and wants expressed in any and every dialogue. Now, after five years of working together, Ann knew Will's story so well that it had become part of her own. It was a story she enjoyed telling. So, she told it again during lunch to everyone at the table, but especially for Jack Grossman and Bob Daringer.

First, she told them that Will Wright was nothing if not pragmatic. He grew up working multiple jobs while completing school with honors. His strong work ethic had come from his grandfather, who served for many years as the president of a local union in his hometown. Will cherished his early experiences with his grandpa.

"Will, my boy," his Grandpa had often said, "When it comes to human relationships, listening is the key to getting the best out of others. People are complicated, and more than a single motivation usually drives them. Nonetheless, if you pay close attention to what other people say, they will begin to tell you what they *really* want most. Once that's clear, it becomes much easier to help them connect their best efforts to what matters most for them and the people around them. People always want to feel like winners, and never like losers."

Grandpa Wright's approach to life was amplified by Will's father and uncle. Both men had grown up to become great athletic coaches. In fact, they coached sports together for over thirty years with a winning percentage of over .800. Although their coaching styles were totally different, they both had an uncanny knack for getting the most out of their players and teams.

Equally impressive was the recurring phenomenon that their former players kept coming back to the local high school gymnasium to do more than reminisce. They came back to actually play basketball, reconnecting with an earlier time when they had learned how to become winners as young men. On any given day, there would be young men, ages twelve to eighteen, participating in practice games alongside former team members in their thirties, forties, and fifties. These were business people, farmers, factory workers, teachers, and even the local mayor. The collage of players came from every walk of life and could not resist coming back year after year, no matter what their lot in life. It's why you may hear Will refer to the Wright Gym, named after his father and uncle, as a resonating core of reciprocity. He's never forgotten the lessons learned from his family mentors and their legend. As a direct result of that nurturing, he has become an effective practitioner and devoted teacher of the amazing power of Reciprocal Results.

Ann Strong observed Jack and Bob during a moment of silence as she finished her storytelling about Will. Then she said, "The gem of wisdom I remember most from Will's stories about his grandpa is this one . . ." She paused, smiling at Will, ". . . do you want to tell them?"

"No. Please go ahead," Will said, feeling a little self-conscious but also filled with a sense of pride.

By all the telltale signs of facial expression and body language—focused eyes, leaning forward, not eating—Jack and Bob were engrossed and ready for Ann's summary gem.

Ann leaned in. There was a slightly lower tone in her voice and she said, "The difference between the human and the divine is that the divine is reciprocal and enabling; the human is hierarchical and controlling."

Jack and Bob slowly nodded, smiling as they considered and appreciated the comment. They looked at Meg and Seth and the other leaders at the table. Everyone seemed to be getting the message and they all seemed to recognize that Ann and Will were more relevant and savvy than met the eye.

"Gems of wisdom from stories of the little red hen and Grandpa Wright," Jack said to laughter all around.

"You're right about great leaders," Bob Daringer said. "They always make things reciprocal. Always."

"What's made the two of you so close over the years besides an obvious complementarity of talent?" Ann asked.

"Reciprocity, without a doubt," Bob responded. "We were both fresh off the college campus, having been highly recruited. Jack was older than me, so he got more offers, but we both chose GE. We had the opportunity to work on major assignments together in GE's fast track program. That's when we learned how important it was to have each other's backs. Our professional and personal relationship became solidified. We became so close that Janey, Jack's wife, actually introduced me to my wife, Amy, at a dinner party at their home. We *must* understand reciprocity because we're both still married."

They all laughed again.

Meg smiled while looking at Seth and the other leaders. "We get it, thank you."

The revolution had definitely started, but would Jack and Bob be able to keep it going? Will asked himself.

As the group reconvened after lunch, all fifty leaders were present. Their body language and facial expressions suggested that they were ready for more.

Will knew from previous experience that, when a breakthrough in perception begins, leaders enter into a new way of thinking that, once experienced, never leaves them. It's like learning how to stand an egg on its end. Once you learn how to do it, it never leaves you.

"Who remembers what we discussed in our first session about too many leaders and organizations getting distracted from Required Results? What distracts them most?"

"Strategy," was the response from several.

"Right. What about Reciprocal Results? What's the major distraction?"

"Leadership methods," said several leaders.

"Yes, too many leaders and organizations get distracted by leadership approaches, development, and recruitment when it comes to Reciprocal Results. The plethora of leadership training models and approaches out there seem to exacerbate the problem. So, let's be clear, the core essence of effective leadership is the ability to create reciprocity in teams and organizations. Winning organizations create winning people, and winning people create winning organizations. A few of us discussed this at lunch. Great leaders throughout history have always sought to make things reciprocal with their key players." Then he put up the following graphic:

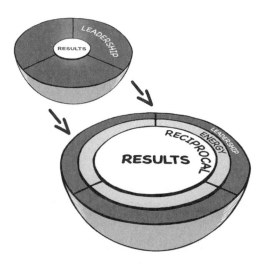

"We overcome the distraction of leadership initiatives by tapping into the abundant energy of Reciprocal Results. When we achieve Reciprocal Results, it provides *prima facie* evidence that we are demonstrating effective leadership. As the slide shows, we need a lever for change between results and leadership to make sure that the glut of leadership theories and practices doesn't distract and disengage us from results. As a lever for change, Reciprocal Results drive us to tap into our real energy and remind us to keep distractions, especially those related to leadership, at bay. Don't misinterpret what I'm saying here. There are many wonderful and wise approaches to leadership that we can and do apply here at Barrington—we just can't let those approaches distract us from the most important part of leadership, which is to create real ownership and buy-in around Required Results . . . and that only happens when we make reciprocity part of the equation. Leadership effectiveness is measured by Reciprocal Results. That's what brings the high release of energy often referred to by academics and behaviorists as discretionary effort. Any questions or comments?"

One leader spoke up. "I agree with what you're saying. It makes such common sense. What I don't understand is how we got here. Why do we let ourselves, our teams, and our organizations get so disconnected from what matters most?"

"Great question," Will said as he went to his computer to find the right graphic to display. "Hopefully these two graphics will bring some clarifying insight to this issue."

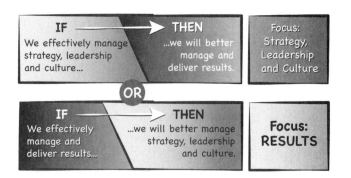

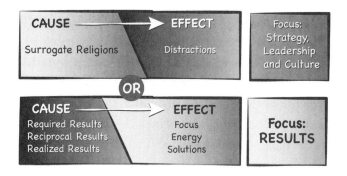

As the slide went up on the screens, one leader, a quick study and rising star in the organization, immediately asked, "Are you saying that all organizations and their leaders have gotten this wrong?"

"I'm saying we've gotten the sequence wrong. How we Lead Results must come first, before strategy, leadership, and culture," Will said with conviction.

Contemplation permeated the room.

Pay dirt was coming, Ann said to herself from the side of the room, just as it had with Rogers.

"Common sense is often not common practice," Will said slowly. "In this case, it's common sense to address the cause, not the effect. But it's so easy to get distracted and lost in the complexity forest, especially if we don't have a compass. The compass we need is a *Cause and Effect* compass to help us find true north. True north is always the cause, never the effect."

What ensued was a hearty discussion about why we so often get cause and effect wrong. Will made it clear that focusing on good strategy, effective leadership, and strong culture as the cause of results actually distracts us from results. We become preoccupied and overwrought with strategy, leadership, and culture. "The more we do it, the worse it gets. Theories and beliefs about strategy, leadership, and culture turn into surrogate religions seeking converts. Distractions increase. Results diminish. It's that simple."

Some heads were nodding, but most of the leaders were still contemplating what Will had said.

"On the other hand," Will continued, "focusing on results as the cause of good strategy, effective leadership, and strong culture puts Required Results first, where they should be. Good strategy, effective leadership, and strong culture become the effects or by-products, never getting overinflated or exaggerated. Distractions and disengagement are minimized. Results flourish. Effectively Leading Results means bringing greater focus, energy, and solutions to bear on what matters most—the needed results themselves. That's why we need a Results Revolution."

As the discussion continued, Will witnessed numerous *aha* moments manifesting themselves. When he asked the leaders to form groups of three to share these insights, the light bulbs turned into epiphanies, and the energy and engagement in the room soared to new heights.

During his debrief of key learnings and takeaways, Will asked Ann to come forward to drive the message home.

"Going forward," Ann stated emphatically, "we will Lead Results first and foremost to lead strategy, leadership, and culture. The reason is simple: getting results right produces the effect of getting strategy, leadership, and culture right. In fact, it's the only thing that does."

Ann then took the opportunity to expand upon the principles of Required Results and Reciprocal Results. "If an organization achieves the Required Results that make it successful, but the people making it happen fail to obtain the personal and professional Reciprocal Results they deserve, the future success and sustainability of that organization will always be in jeopardy. Why? Because winning organizations cannot continue to win without ensuring that every employee responsible for that success is also winning, not in a trickle-down fashion but in a direct way. Building winners goes hand in hand with winning teams, business units, and companies. The secret to moving an organization from good to great, and keeping it there, lies in continually creating great outcomes for the organization, teams, and people who deliver the results . . . no matter what.

"How? In the simplest, most basic cause and effect terms, achieving and sustaining extraordinary results requires making results reciprocal. Reciprocal Results occur when the desired results of *both* the organization and the individual are achieved. That's what we have to get right. Think about it. The work environment is the one place where we fail to effectively apply reciprocity. We apply the principle of reciprocity to customers, suppliers, shareholders, and communities, but not to employees.

"For years, we have known that people perform at their best when their individual and collective achievements are valued and rewarded. Attempting to convince people that they are valued and rewarded on any basis other than Reciprocal Results doesn't work, at least not in the long run. So, why not truly partner with each other around Reciprocal Results?"

One leader asked, "Are there companies that are actually making results reciprocal?"

"Yes," Ann said excitedly. "In fact, when you examine

the data, Reciprocal Results have always been an abiding hallmark of perennially successful organizations. These are companies that achieve industry dominance and economic leadership, making it possible for them to reinvest in the business and their people at a rate that was two to ten times higher than their competitors. For example, Procter & Gamble, Starbucks, and Google have consistently outperformed their competitors by ten to twenty times as measured by market value. These organizations regularly show up on lists of most admired companies, best places to work, and blue-chip investments. Both have learned, often the hard way, how to make results reciprocal.

"Procter & Gamble has maintained the respect of millions of people throughout the world through its profound respect for individuals. The company's high level of trust facilitates astonishingly open and candid discussions about mistakes, failures, and improvement . . . but it doesn't come easily. Such open, self-critiquing discussions make P&G employees feel vulnerable while at the same time spurring them on to more learning, improvement, outstanding performance, and personal satisfaction.

"Starbucks' 'pour your heart into it' leadership has led to a working environment where people are encouraged and incented to take accountability for dreaming and growing and making Starbucks ever better. Employees see a direct correlation between great ideas and great results for both the individual and the company. It's no surprise that Starbucks gets labeled 'the best first job in the world.'

"For the past several years, Google has been number one on *Fortune's* list of 100 Best Companies to Work For. Google employees, now over 75,000 worldwide, consistently give the company ratings of 95 to 98 percent when asked to rate the organization and its leaders in the following criteria: 1) Great Challenges, 2) Great Atmosphere, 3) Great Rewards, 4) Great Pride, 5) Great Communication, and 6) Great Bosses.

"None of these companies is perfect, but all three are working hard to create and maintain a Reciprocal Results environment for their employees . . . like the one we're trying to create here at Barrington."

From the rapt attention in the room, Ann knew that, together with Will, she was forging an enduring connection with the top fifty leaders. Barrington's very own Results Revolution was now showing momentum.

They took a fifteen-minute break. During the break, Jack and Bob nodded their approval. The group seemed ready for the next step.

After the leaders returned from break, Will divided them into natural teams around each of Ann's direct reports. He asked a member of each team to retrieve a flip chart from the back of the room.

When they were ready, Will gave his instructions. "For the next fifteen minutes, I'd like you to engage in a vigorous discussion about how Barrington's leadership, methods, development, and recruitment are linked to, related to, or associated with Reciprocal Results and the heightened energy levels that arise from true reciprocity. Use the flip chart to capture all of the connections. As you did with strategy in the last session, record key words on your flip chart. Fill up at least one page. You've got fifteen minutes."

After fifteen minutes, Will had a spokesperson from each team summarize his or her group's experience. In most cases, the teams had filled up two flip charts with connections. This time, when Will asked the entire group to capture the primary take away from this exercise, it was Rachel Radcliffe, CHRO, who provided the best summary.

"What struck me . . . like a lightning bolt, actually . . . was that almost everything we do under the umbrella of leadership development and recruitment is about drawing the best out of our people, which is what Reciprocal Results does from the beginning . . . only faster and better. We really have been making this much more difficult and complicated than it needs to be."

There was an immediate round of applause in the room.

They get it.

To deepen their understanding and ability to apply Reciprocal Results (in other words, dealing with real wants and motivations instead of building armor against greater transparency), Will introduced what would become a breakthrough exercise: What Matters Most to Your Boss, Personally & Professionally. The purpose of this exercise was to have each team member become intimately familiar with what mattered most to his or her boss, so the leaders remained in their natural teams.

For the next thirty minutes of intense focus on reciprocity, everyone had to revisit their understanding of and commitment to reciprocity in ways they hadn't experienced before. *What does my boss really want? Is the reciprocity between what's expected and what's promised both equitable and balanced? What does true "value add" look like for your boss and what does he or she want in return?*

The exercise allowed many people to deepen their

understanding of their bosses as well as the process of making everything reciprocal. The *aha* moments were heartfelt and pervasive throughout all of the natural teams. Suddenly, the personal and professional Reciprocal Results for each of Ann's direct reports became transparent and alive. There wasn't a leader in the room who hadn't learned something new about his or her boss. The interesting thing was that most of the more successful and promising leaders in the group already knew a lot about their bosses.

After hearing a brief summary of the exercise outcomes from each team, Will introduced the final exercise of the day with the following prelude: "This next exercise will help you to better understand the motivations and desires of the other members of your team." He asked them to remain in their natural teams once again. There were four to seven leaders per team. Each person would have ten minutes to present and elaborate on his or her personal and professional Reciprocal Results while the other team members listened and recorded notes in their workbooks.

The next two hours were, according to Jack Grossman, "nothing short of miraculous." Barrington Corp's top fifty leaders began sharing real expectations from their professional and personal Reciprocal Results. While such needs and desires had been discussed on occasion, they had never been so fully expressed, explained, or mutually understood. A new bond was developing among the leadership team . . . producing a Results Partnership they had never experienced before.

"In one sentence, how would you describe the experience you've had in the past couple of hours?" Will asked the group.

A flurry of responses came one after the other:

"Very eye opening."

"I didn't realize how much I didn't know."

"It felt liberating to be so transparent with each other."

"I didn't think I'd ever experience something like this at work."

"There's a new level of connectedness in this group that I haven't felt before."

"Our Required Results just took on a whole new level of meaning and passion."

"I've never been more motivated about work."

It was 5:20 p.m., when Will turned the room over to Ann for a wrap-up. The group of leaders had indeed achieved a breakthrough. It felt exhilarating and empowering.

Ann told the leaders that the most important session was yet to come. Session three would be held in two weeks to address making sure all of the Required Results and Reciprocal Results get realized. Similar to the last session, she gave a homework assignment to every leader in the room: their assignment was to meet with his or her direct supervisor during the next fourteen days to review and confirm their Results Commitment. It was a three-part commitment to (1) deliver on your individual Results Map, (2) deliver on your personal and professional Reciprocal Results, and (3) help everyone on your teams (the team you're a member of and the team you lead) to remain committed to achieving both Required and Reciprocal Results.

Once again, there were a few questions that she and Will answered quickly and concisely. But both of them knew the Results Commitment would provoke more robust conversations during the next two weeks.

Ann closed the session with the following story of her former company, where she served as CEO for five years. "When I became CEO of Waring Enterprises six years ago, I immediately recognized that the company had a results problem. At the time I joined them, the $1 billion consumer products company had become a market leader in several niche markets. But the organization's ten thousand employees were struggling to sustain the company's market leadership, grow profits, build alignment around top priorities, and demonstrate real ownership for continuous improvement. I was charged with preserving the company's eroding market leadership positions, maximizing the company's growth and driving profitability to new heights.

"But the results weren't right. We weren't focusing on the right Required Results and we weren't committed to delivering Reciprocal Results, so we began to seriously rethink about how we needed to change to win as individuals and as an organization. Will Wright helped us walk through this same process of rethinking results. The rest is history.

"In just five years, the company posted remarkable results: revenues grew by more than 100% with profitability increasing more than 250%. Market leadership was maintained, strengthened, and created anew. In November of last year, Waring Enterprises was acquired by General Electric for approximately six times revenue. By all accounts, it was an extraordinary turnaround because we learned how to get results right by (1) focusing on the Required Results, (2) energizing people through Reciprocal Results, and (3) staying in solutions mode until all of the results were realized—and that's what our third session will be about . . . Realized Results."

As Jack Grossman and Bob Daringer left the session, they raised both their hands, Jack with double thumbs up and Bob with nine and one half-bent fingers out stretched. They were both smiling and nodding at Will and Ann. The Results Revolution was gaining steam.

14

THE ANCHOR

Rogers Barrington sat in his 54th floor office watching the sun rise over Lake Michigan and second-guessing himself about Ann Strong and Will Wright and their Results Revolution. During the past ten days, he'd received several troubling phone calls from long-time employees and influential family members. All of them were complaining about the same thing: the methods being employed by the company's newest CEO and her Harvard professor. Their complaints ranged from freezing compensation to ignoring internal operations to wasting time in offsite meetings to being obsessed with results training to violating John Rogers Barrington's values. He'd been tempted to intervene by talking directly to Ann's direct reports but had decided to wait until after this morning's meeting with her and Will Wright. He just didn't understand the growing unrest or this negative, unsolicited feedback. He'd even been tempted to begin talks with a few CEO recruiters. If he needed to pull the plug on the fourth CEO in eight years, he was going to do it earlier rather than later . . . regardless of how sickening the thought was to him. His grandfather's values could not and would not be violated . . . not on his watch. Nothing mattered more than preserving the light of the family's resolve. But he acknowledged that he might be overreacting.

When Ann and Will arrived to give him an update before their next offsite, Rogers was pacing back and forth in front of the windows overlooking Lake Michigan. Spring was beautiful and exhilarating in The Windy City, but right now Rogers was feeling only a return to uncertainty and torment.

"Please, sit down," Rogers said as Ann and Will entered his office.

Ann immediately sensed that Rogers was troubled about something and she was never one to dance around the obvious. "You seem upset . . . everything okay?"

"No, actually," Rogers said while walking over to the sitting area where Ann and Will were now sitting. Rogers remained standing. "I have received a number of disturbing calls in the past few days from shareholders and employees asking me to shut down your Results Revolution and send Mr. Wright here back to Harvard."

Will sat back in his seat on the sofa. This was Ann's issue to address. He would speak only when and if requested.

Ann sat up straight on the edge of her seat in the overstuffed chair, her chin raised and eyes intense. "I told you to expect some backlash," she said.

Rogers stood motionless waiting for her to continue, but she didn't. Silence lingered in the office for several seconds.

"I didn't expect key family members to be so vehement in accusing me of allowing our grandfather's values and principles to be betrayed. I think it launched me into a nowhere land of second-guessing."

"I'm sorry that you've had to experience that. I know how important your grandfather's values are to you and the family," Ann expressed sympathetically. Then she paused for a moment, intensity and resolve returning to her eyes. "I don't mean to sound defensive, but you and your family need to acknowledge the reality that most of Barrington's 30,000 employees are currently violating every one of your grandfather's values."

Rogers took a seat in the overstuffed chair opposite Ann. The three of them sat in a triangle around the large coffee table. "You know that's not how the people who are calling me see it."

"That makes sense because I don't think they see it like I do. Besides revitalizing this company's financial position over the past year, I have painstakingly assessed its work environment, organizational culture, value system, and leaders. Unfortunately, your grandfather's values and principles are not being lived or applied at Barrington Corp. There is no integrity in failing to connect the dots between what you do every day and its impact on what matters most to the company. The majority of people in this company don't know how to demonstrate this sort of integrity . . . people in most organizations don't know how. Nonetheless, their lack of understanding and know-how is undermining you, me, and the company's leaders."

Rogers was stunned. This was not the reaction or response that he expected. *Ann seems irritated,* he thought.

Ann continued, "There is no respect in talking behind our backs, stirring up discord and dissent in secret, and fueling the rumor mill with inaccurate and damaging information. Assuming the worst about everything is not healthy.

"There is no fairness in allowing some people to give their all while other people give only a portion of their all. Most of the people in this company are giving only a portion of their all and it's not fair. Most of this company's employees do not demonstrate trustworthiness in this regard. However, one redeeming factor is that, in most cases, they don't even realize it.

"There is no superior customer service delivered by organizations whose employees feel entitled to their jobs and benefits regardless of whether or not the company's customers are satisfied with the company's products and services. Most of Barrington's employees fail to consistently demonstrate a real understanding of or commitment to superior customer service. These are just some of the reasons why we're in the middle of a Results Revolution . . . and the pressure on you to throw in the towel is going to get worse before it gets better."

Rogers stared pensively at Ann before responding. "I don't disagree with you, Ann. We've discussed this before, but without the sharpness or clarity you just provided. Please send me an email me with what you just articulated . . . I'll use it," he said in a conciliatory tone. "That being said, why are there leaders complaining that your workshops are redundant and a Results Revolution is overkill?"

"Because they think they get it, but they don't," Ann said immediately. "Have you talked to any of the top fifty leaders directly?"

"No, I chose not to until we had this talk."

"I appreciate that, but I *want* you to talk to them because what you're hearing now is second or third hand interpretation and innuendo at best. During the last session, several of the younger leaders questioned whether they needed to stay for the entire workshop because they thought they had completely gotten the message about results. We had lunch with them during the session, but it was Jack and Bob, not me or Will, who convinced them to stay."

"What did they say?"

"They repeated what every strong and effective leader eventually learns. People will never consistently give their all without also getting what they want and need. There has to be reciprocity. The leader's primary role is to ensure it, which means creating alignment between what matters most to the organization and what matters most to the individual. Great leaders find a way to satisfy their customers, their employees, their shareholders, and every other stakeholder that has an impact on the success and sustainability of the enterprise. That's what some of our younger leaders weren't grasping. Jack and Bob helped them see that there was more to results and reciprocity than they were seeing."

"Then why am I getting these calls?"

"Before lunch in our last session, I told them they could leave with no repercussions. I'm sure that word has gotten out. People interpret things the way they want. No one's happy about the new compensation policy. I'm sure some of the leaders are still working through their level of commitment to the Results Revolution."

"So, what's next?"

"Our next session is in two days. It's the anchor to what we're doing because now we have to realize all the results we've been talking about for the past several weeks," Ann said as she handed him a sheet of paper with the final shift that needed to occur for the Results Revolution to be realized.

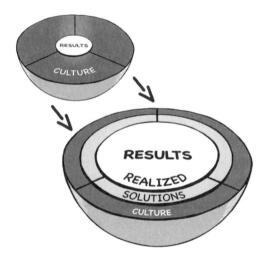

Ann continued as Rogers looked at the graphic. "When business leaders attempt the sort of transformation we're desiring, they usually turn their attention to culture change. But culture change can become a huge distraction to finding the necessary solutions to actually realize results. At the end of the day, the most effective cultures are founded upon realizing results. That's what will anchor us to what matters most. Addressing results first and foremost ensures that your culture change efforts are aligned with achieving the results that matter most."

She had done it again—allayed his concerns and lessened his uncertainty.

"Okay, Ann. I'll take care of the family. You make sure these leaders are behind you. If any of them aren't, I want to know about it. We can't afford any dissenters among the top fifty."

"Thank you, Rogers. I promise you that what we're doing will return Barrington to greatness. Without consciously recognizing it, the people who contacted you and members of your family may be hiding their own agendas behind your grandfather's values. The only way to effectively address that is to shift our daily attention to the results we must deliver. I promised you a Results Revolution and I intend to achieve one."

"Despite my occasional anxieties, I believe you, Ann," Rogers said with emotion. Then he turned to Will, who had been quiet since he arrived. "Thank you, Will, for what you're doing here. I support both of you . . . this revolution must happen."

"Thank you," Will said graciously.

15

SUNSHINE AND SOLUTIONS

Ann kicked off this session by making it clear that she expected everyone in the room to deliver on *all* of their agreed upon Required Results and Reciprocal Results, organizational, team, position, and personal/professional. All of them were interrelated and crucial to Barrington's success.

"That is the essence of Reciprocal Results—both the individual and the organization must achieve their results for success to be whole and sustainable. It's also the core lesson of the little red hen. . . sharing the bread equitably, but *only* with those who help make it and based on their respective contributions, impact, and value add. We need everyone in this organization delivering Required Results and Reciprocal

Results for the organization, their teams, and themselves. That's the only way we'll achieve a Results Revolution. Today is about how to make that happen," Ann said as she turned the session over to Will.

Will then built upon the moment by retelling the story of the little red hen and describing what he called "the culmination"—creating a Results Revolution. "This is where the rubber meets the road. This is how a Results Revolution actually becomes a *revolution*." He put up the slide with the central model and offered a simple explanation of Realized Results. "Realized Results are about one thing: sustaining a daily focus on required and Reciprocal Results that are *not* on the path to becoming realized. Why? To immediately and effectively find solutions to get those results on path to becoming realized. That will become the new norm of our revolutionized culture."

The first exercise of the day introduced the Results Dialogue—an exchange of feedback focused on overcoming obstacles and removing barriers that could jeopardize the delivery of Required Results or Reciprocal Results. The purpose of the Results Dialogue was to keep everyone on the path to achieving results: for the organization as a whole, for each team, within each team position, and for every individual, personally and professionally.

The exercise began with Will asking the group to get into natural teams once again. Then, he explained that this exercise was designed to challenge traditional perspectives and habits around getting to results. It was also intended to build proficiency in the Results Dialogue.

As the leaders gathered into their groups, Will walked over to Jack Grossman.

"Still at a ten?" Will asked.

"I am."

"This exercise will keep you there."

"The only thing that will keep me at a ten is the achievement of results."

"Exactly." Will smiled, knowing that most senior executives talked about Realized Results all the time, but he also knew that they often failed to engage in real, ongoing dialogue to address the tough questions, obstacles, and barriers that might jeopardize the achievement of Realized Results. Sadly, too many senior leaders expect desired outcomes to happen because they emphasize them all the time. Their unstated assumption is: *if you have the right people in place, they will deliver on their promises . . . otherwise you don't have the right people.*

When the leaders were settled in their groups, Will

described the common process of accounting for performance. "Whenever desired results are not achieved or are clearly identified as *not on path* to being achieved, this triggers an ugly roasting of one or more leaders who become fall guys. The ironic aspect of such age-old rituals is that, by the time the *accounting* occurs, prospects for a results turnaround are often unlikely."

Silence hung over the ballroom.

One leader finally spoke, "When my numbers are good, the sessions are just as nerve-racking and time-consuming. Frankly, they're always a pain in the ass."

There were a few nervous chuckles along with a fair amount of fidgeting and a lot of craning necks. Unfortunately, it was an indication of another barrier to success. Was the group of leaders in a better place than it had been in the first two sessions? *Absolutely,* Will said to himself. *But we're not where we need to be. Not yet.*

Instead of reacting to his concern, Will calmly asked the next logical question, "What about when the numbers are not good?"

"It's incredibly embarrassing," said one leader.

Many of the heads in the room were bent down. No one seemed to want to make eye contact with Will or anyone else for that matter. This was not a topic they wanted to talk about, despite their positive and transparent experiences in the past two sessions. Will was not surprised or daunted. He was well aware that a robust, ongoing Results Dialogue was the only thing that would ultimately change each leader's mindset and beliefs about accounting for and reporting on progress toward Required Results and Reciprocal Results.

The leader continued, "Everyone knows there's going

to be a ruthless interrogation with no recourse for those on the hot seat."

"So, as a leader, you know this negative experience is coming even before you go into the meeting?" Will asked.

"Of course we do," the leader said, becoming more emboldened with each interchange. "Everybody in this room knows that . . . and, in the spirit of openness and transparency, it sucks the energy out of everyone, big time."

Dead silence filled the Avenues Ballroom. The leader who had just completed the public exchange with Will was one of Stephanie Masters' direct reports. Stephanie, along with several other senior leaders, was visibly surprised by her direct report's unabashed candor.

Will stared around the room. His voice was calm and resolute, "So let me get this straight. You know before you even go into the meeting what's coming and how bad it's going to hurt?"

Another leader who seemed as if she was about to explode jumped out of her seat. "Yeah—we get our best documentation and explanations together. Sometimes we're pulling data right up to the last second before we have to present. But we know we're going to get whacked."

There were some red faces in the group and general body language that communicated *let's move on.*

However, Will consciously ignored the body language and pushed forward with what was apparently starting to feel, for most people in the room, like an annoying line of questioning. "What does it feel like to get whacked?"

"It's like getting punished twice," said another leader. "One beating is self-imposed and happens when you face your own actual break down in delivering results before you have to report. The second beating happens during the meeting when you are obligated to publically admit the failure. It's simply a horrible experience."

Another leader continued, "Then the discussion turns to the loser's failure in leadership. It's humiliating . . . like that old television show Branded . . . they rip off your medals and break your sword before you get drummed out of the Corps in absolute disgrace."

Will began walking around the circled groups as he continued to peel the proverbial onion. "I know this is frustrating, but you obviously have a great deal of negative energy around this issue. Why not simply identify the gap or shortfall when it happens, fix it before the presentation, and avoid the punishment?"

There were numerous double takes.

"Are you kidding?" said one leader. "We spend most days fighting fires."

Another leader piped in, "We're too damn busy trying to get all of our work done to think about the results until we absolutely have to . . . and there is always a chance—"

"—What sort of chance?" Will interrupted.

"A chance that things will improve." The leader glared at Will. "We've got good people here, but it always seems like the real objective is to publically embarrass someone . . . getting that pound of flesh while putting the fear of God in everyone else."

"Given the looks on your faces, this sounds about right," Will said. "So why don't your direct reports let you know that things are going south as soon as it starts to happen?"

A leader in the back spoke up. "Three reasons—one is

fear, two is that there are too many other things that have to get done, and three is there's no reward for speaking up. In fact, you might be indirectly punished for it."

Another leader from the side shouted, "That's the understatement of the decade!"

More snickers filled the room.

Will quickly interrupted. "What is the fear about—precisely?" Will wasn't about to stop until he got to the root cause and core problem. Suddenly, there were four rapid-fire responses from different leaders.

"Fear of appearing to be unsupportive of the leader or the team by raising the red flag."

"Fear of looking like a whistle-blower."

"Fear of breaking ranks."

"Fear of coming across as disloyal."

"Sorry, but I still don't think we've gotten to the crux of the matter," Will said. "Can you please go deeper and be more specific?"

"Call it the Emperor's New Clothes, call it 'kill the messenger' syndrome, a career limiting move, or whatever . . . the perceived reality around here is that if you step up, you could be committing political or career suicide."

Will paused and surveyed the room. Most of the leaders appeared to agree that this was the reality and, worse yet, that it was unresolvable. "Help me. Why are the top fifty leaders of this company choosing to reinforce the fear? I am getting the distinct impression that while nearly everyone in the room would like to change this reality, no one believes he or she can. Am I right?"

"How else do we hold people accountable for the results we have committed to deliver?" Stephanie Masters asked.

Will calmly responded with another question, "Would you like a different approach?"

"We would," Stephanie returned. "But we want an approach that will make things better, not worse than they are."

"Okay. What would it look like if we totally revolutionized the way we Lead Results?"

Trey Gorski, a leader who reported to Jack Grossman and had not yet spoken in open forum, said, "We'd have to turn everything upside down."

"What do you mean, Trey? What would it look like to turn everything upside down?"

"We'd have to look at emerging results much earlier in the process, before it's too late to course correct."

Will turned to the larger group and asked, "What do you think?"

"We also have to make it less about punishing and more about figuring out how to win," said another leader.

"Agreed. The only way we make it less threatening is to be focused on overcoming barriers and not on placing blame. That means we have to be developing course corrections more often, at least early enough to make a difference, just like Trey said. That's the only way we make this positive rather negative."

Another leader weighed in, "Everyone would have to agree to the new approach and be willing to implement it."

"We'd have to make sure the old approach didn't creep back in."

Maureen Dimitriou, VP of Talent Development and one of CHRO Rachel Radcliffe's direct reports, weighed in next. "If we actually did something like this and everyone truly bought in . . ." She paused for a moment. ". . . It could put us ahead of the performance curve for once . . . instead of always being behind it."

Then the CFO, James Grand, weighed in, "If we could move from reacting to missed results and putting people on the hot seat too late, to anticipating missed results and putting people on the path to solutions continuously and much earlier, it would truly be a revolution worth waging."

Ann recapped the commentary. "So, here's what I'm hearing: if we turn our pursuit of results into a positive, ahead of the curve, early detection, helpful rather than harmful, solutions-oriented experience, you're all in?"

This time the "yes" was both resounding and deafening. Jack Grossman and Bob Daringer were the first two to stand in what became a standing ovation.

Ann smiled broadly while nodding her agreement and appreciation. She looked over at Will with a gesture for him to continue. They now had the green light they were looking for.

Will immediately put three questions on the screen. "These three simple questions will help you practice and socialize the Results Dialogue.

Results Dialogue Questions

1. What Required or Reciprocal Result concerns you most today?

2. What are your most promising solutions for getting this result back on path?

3. What else needs to happen and how can I help?

Review your Results Map and Results Commitment to
identify the one result that concerns you the most today. It
might be a Required Result at the organization, team, or
position level. Or, it might be a Reciprocal Result at the
personal/professional level for you, your boss, or one of your
peers. Once you've made your pick, stand up and find a
partner inside or outside your team."

When everyone was partnered up, Will gave them
additional instructions. "You'll have three minutes with each
partner, which means you each have a minute and a half to
ask your partner the three Results Dialogue questions. We're
going to do this ten times with ten different partners. I'll let
you know when three minutes are up and give you thirty
seconds to find your next partner beforehand. Think of this
as ten lightening rounds or speed dating with a Results
Dialogue."

After the wise cracks died down, the clock started. For
the next forty minutes, the room was aflutter with Results
Dialogues. Focus was sharp, energy was high, and solutions
were flowing.

To debrief the exercise, Will first asked the group,
"Was this a valuable experience?"

There was a resounding, "Yes."

Will's second question was, "Can you see yourself
doing this every day?"

Another resounding, "Yes."

Then, Will asked, "Why? . . . Why did you find this

valuable and why would you be willing to do it every day, even multiple times a day?"

The responses came fast and furiously:

> *It's easy.*
> *It's non-threatening.*
> *Makes you think.*
> *Opens us up to each other.*
> *Allows us to help.*
> *Gets to the heart of the matter.*
> *It's positive, not negative.*
> *Keeps ahead of the curve.*
> *Focuses on solutions and the path forward.*
> *There's no judgement or critique.*
> *It's so simple.*

"Is there anything you would change or add to these three Results Dialogue questions?" Will asked.

"I think once we get used to doing it daily, we'll make it our own, and it will evolve. We just have to guard against slipping back to the old way."

Another leader added, "The key is to have lots of Results Dialogues going on all the time."

"Exactly. I agree with both comments," Will said.

"What do we do when we see another leader not making the progress they need to make, but they're not asking me to engage in a Results Dialogue? We don't want to go back to the old hot seat approach."

"What do you think, team?" Will asked.

Bob Daringer immediately stood up and began speaking with a defiant tone. "If any of you think or perceive or have even the slightest inkling, for any reason whatsoever, that I'm not going to meet or exceed any of my required or Reciprocal Results—"

A sudden spike in laughter cut Bob off.

Bob was grinning ear to ear. He'd set them up and Will loved it. As the laughter died down, Bob's face turned solemn with a resolved expression that he held for several seconds before speaking again in a soft even tone.

"—if any of you have the slightest inkling that I'm not going to meet or exceed any of my results, I want you to hear about it . . . I want to talk about it . . . I need to see what you see . . . I'll do the same for you."

Will nodded his admiration and approval as Bob sat down. The reversal in emotion that Bob had just exhibited could not have been executed more perfectly or more sincerely. Now, Will waited along with the rest of the group to see how Jack Grossman, who was now standing, would respond. Bob was a hard act to follow.

Tangible uncertainty permeated the air. Would Jack be funny or solemn? As it turned out, he was piercingly insightful.

"When we started this process, I was at a two on a scale of one to ten. I told my wife it was time to buy our retirement villa in Italy."

The ballroom erupted in laughter once again.

"However," Jack continued, "I moved to a six after the first session. Then, to my utter surprise, I moved to a ten after the second session. This morning, Will asked me if I was still at a ten. I told him I was. Then, he told me that today's session would keep me at a ten. I told him that the only thing that would keep me at a ten was the achievement of the results themselves. Will's response was 'exactly,' which I didn't fully understand until just now, when Bob stood up and delivered his emotional turnabout."

Attention was rapt as the group waited for Jack's punch line.

"This dialogue about the results that matter most to us—personally and professionally, in teams and organizationally—must become our most important daily priority. But it has to be real, true dialogue." Jack turned to face Will Wright. "I'm now at a twelve, because I can actually envision how this simple Results Dialogue, applied effectively and constantly, will take us to the finish line, again and again and again. I now get all of it. This is the heart of the Results Revolution."

The room exploded with another standing ovation.

Jack's breakthrough 'aha' had come earlier than expected, Will thought, as he stood to applaud the man who had once been his toughest critic. Their eyes met in mutual respect. *Today is going to be incredible.*

Will remained standing as the applause subsided and everyone sat down again. "Thank you, Jack, Bob and Ann for making this a most remarkable workshop . . . and it will only get better from here."

There was more applause as the group broke for lunch.

Setting the stage for embedding the Results Dialogue into the DNA of these fifty leaders was Will's challenge for the afternoon.

16

ALIGNING CULTURE

When the leaders returned from a splendid buffet lunch of high-end Mexican cuisine, Will moved quickly. "It's time to talk about distractions again. Think back to our first session together. What's the biggest distraction to Required Results?"

"Strategy," came the shout from several leaders.

"Right! And why?"

Several leaders raised their hands. Will pointed to one of them.

"We tend to get bogged down in details around strategic positioning, competitive maneuvering, and initiatives tracking, which causes us to take our eyes off the Required Results. I also think we spend so much time trying to get the strategy right that we short change execution."

"Perfect. What about Reciprocal Results?"

"Leadership," was the response from several leaders.

"Right again. Why leadership?"

Again, several hands went up. Will pointed to someone at the back of the room.

"There are so many different leadership philosophies and practices being applied today that we lose sight of the single most important thing about leadership, which is to make sure that everyone is on board and committed to delivering the Required Results. People want to feel valued and appropriately rewarded for their contributions. I don't see how we could do this more effectively than through reciprocity. And, that can't happen unless there's mutual benefit and a real Results Partnership committed to delivering Reciprocal Results."

"Yes," Will said. "Again, don't get me wrong, enormous benefit can be derived from today's leadership philosophies and practices. We just have to focus on creating Reciprocal Results first. When we do, all of that leadership wisdom complements what we're doing rather than distracts us from what matters most."

The group of leaders seemed genuinely pleased with themselves. *It's sinking in.*

"Okay, when it comes to Realized Results, too many leaders and organizations get distracted by culture. Does that surprise you?"

"No," said one leader and then went on to clarify her comment. "When we focus on culture change without first getting rooted in results, we risk spending too much time and effort trying to change the way people think and feel and act rather than realizing results."

"Nicely done," Will said, as he put up a slide similar to

the ones he'd used in previous sessions on the screens at the front of the room.

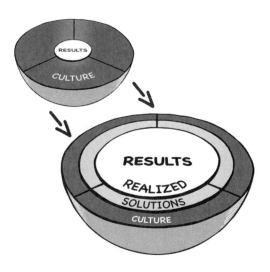

"We overcome the distraction and disengagement associated with culture by making sure that our culture is aligned with finding solutions that bring Realized Results. No matter how you define culture—values and beliefs, norms and routines, symbols and language, patterns and practices, networks and mapping—all of it must be grounded in and aligned with finding solutions to achieve results. Translated into action that means that every issue, problem, obstacle, set-back, barrier, unanticipated occurrence, or act of God must be approached with a solution mindset directed at realizing results. Amazon is a great example. Everyone in the company is searching on a daily basis for new solutions that will maintain and expand the greatest selling platform the world has ever known.

"In the end, Realized Results are the only true

evidence of a healthy and highly effective organizational culture. Our collective resolve and commitment to deliver Realized Results represents the most important belief or norm of a strong culture. Once again, the graphic shows a lever for change positioned between results and culture to make sure that all culture change efforts are always focused on realizing the results that matter most. Culture is shaped most by the organization's Realized Results, and we need to use that reality to drive continuous solutions. Any questions or comments?"

There was only silence. But this time Will wasn't concerned. *They're totally getting it,* he thought to himself.

"Let's get into your natural teams again . . . and you'll need a flipchart."

The leaders responded quickly. Each natural team circled their chairs while sending one of their ranks to get a flip chart.

One of the leaders called out, "Fifteen minutes of rigorous discussion, right?"

"Yes," Will bellowed as laughter filled the room.

When they had settled in, Will continued. "Take fifteen minutes to discuss how Barrington's culture is linked to, related to, or associated with Realized Results. In other words, what are the beliefs, norms, and habits in our culture that have an impact on whether we actually realize our results? Keywords are all you have to record. Fill at least one page."

Fifteen minutes later, Will had a spokesperson from each group summarize his or her group's experience. Similar to the previous discussions around strategy and leadership, the connections between culture and Realized Results were profuse. When Will asked the entire group to capture the primary take away from this exercise, he was not surprised that Jack Grossman was the one to nail it.

"Every time we've done this exercise it's become more and more clear how distracted we get by wrapping ourselves up in strategy, leadership, and culture without keeping results in first place. In this case, it's very clear-cut . . . the organization's culture either facilitates Realized Results or it doesn't. Once we establish our Required Results and our Reciprocal Results, they have to become Realized Results. That has to become our culture. If you think about it, the results an organization achieves always create the experiences that most consistently shape the culture. If we want to change Barrington's culture, we need to realize these results we've been working on for the past month."

The immediate applause was in part because of the group's esteem for Jack but also because of the group's blossoming alignment.

"Thank you, Jack. The focus and energy of this team are unmistakable. Now, let's turn that focus and energy into solutions that produce the results we want." Mindsets had been unfrozen, beliefs were suspended, and transformation was afoot and tangibly visible. Both he and Ann were thrilled.

Will continued, "Here's how it works. Anything that concerns you requires at least one Results Dialogue with someone at Barrington. Everyone must commit to initiating at least one Results Dialogue every day, which means you always need to be ready to answer the first question: What Required or Reciprocal Result concerns you most today?"

Based on the looks of acknowledgement, affirmative nods and *aha* facial expressions, Will's message was landing.

They get it.

The exercise that followed began with each of Ann's nine direct reports conducting a group Results Dialogue with a slightly modified set of questions:

Results Dialogue Questions (Group)

1. What Required or Reciprocal Result concern us most as a team? (focus on top three)

2. What are our most promising solutions for getting these results back on path?

3. What else needs to happen and how can we help each other?

Thirty minutes later, there were plenty of questions.

"How often should we be doing this group version?"

"As often as you need to. In general, you should try to have at least one Results Dialogue every day and at least one group Results Dialogue once a week."

"What if someone's personal/professional result gets identified in the group Results Dialogue?"

"Great question. It should happen a lot. We need to have open, transparent conversations about what matters most. Reciprocal Results are a vital part of what matters most."

"What if the group Results Dialogue becomes uncomfortable? I mean, what if someone gets defensive?" asked one leader.

"Explain your perception, emphasizing your intent to

help that team member be successful. If that doesn't work, then ask them to articulate their discomfort. The Results Dialogue must continue until all parties are satisfied that there's a viable path of action for getting the result back on path."

"What if we're afraid the person impacted will get upset, so we don't raise it?"

"Don't be afraid."

There was nervous laughter.

Will continued, "Seriously, none of this will produce the Results Revolution we want if we don't talk about what matters most all the time. Remember what Bob Daringer said this morning?"

They remembered but waited for Will to repeat it.

"If any of you have the slightest inkling that I'm not going to meet or exceed any of my required or Reciprocal Results, I want to hear about . . . I want to talk about it . . . I need to see what you see . . . I'll do the same for you."

"Thank you, Bob," shouted Stephanie Masters from the back of the ballroom where she was standing.

The applause was spontaneous.

Will grinned broadly. "If you ever need to be reminded of how important this is, check in with Bob."

Hoots and hollers filled the ballroom.

After addressing a few more questions, Will happily judged the team's mood as passionately and intellectually curious. They were ready and willing to learn more and get better at the Results Dialogue. *The team is in a very good place,* Will thought to himself.

During the rest of the day, Will facilitated the team's skill development by practicing and debriefing application of the Results Dialogue. He began by asking Bob Daringer to join him at the front of the room.

"Are you willing to role play with me?"

"Absolutely," Bob returned.

"Let's assume that you and I are on the same team and that I perceive you will have to make changes to meet or exceed your Reciprocal Results."

"Easy."

After the ripple of laughter, attention was riveted.

"I start my Results Dialogue informally, because I've been doing it every day for a while. I begin by saying something like, 'Based on our recent conversations, you seem to be struggling with one or more of your Reciprocal Results. How can I help?'"

"My team's lack of experience is killing me. I love my expanded role but I'm logging eighty-plus hours per week with no end in sight. You know my wife, she gets it, but it's killing her too. Neither one of us is around for each other or the kids."

"Nice role play," Will said.

There were more hoots and hollers as Bob ceremoniously bowed to the audience.

"So, your work-life balance result is in jeopardy?" Will asked.

"You got it," Bob responded. "Along with at least one of my team member's Required Results."

"Damn . . . you're screwed!"

The ballroom popped with guffaws.

When the laughter subsided, Will said, "Seriously, here's where I would go with Bob at this point . . . First, I would acknowledge that better work-life balance would enable his pursuit of a more meaningful relationship with his spouse and children. Which means, we have to get his imbalance addressed soon. Then, I'd try to help him find one to three solutions that he could immediately implement to address his situation. Solutions must be the end game of every Results Dialogue."

Based on their facial expressions the leaders seemed to be in sync with what Will was saying.

"Okay, let's continue with the role play," Will said as he looked back at Bob, who was standing five feet away from him and smiling. "Which member of your team is causing you the greatest grief? Or currently demanding the most from you?"

"Several of them are very challenging, but Sarah consumes the bulk of my mentoring time. She's highly talented and will be a great group president someday, but right now she's draining me. She's not grounded in the industry, she lacks strategic perspective, she's a bully to her people, and she makes impulsive decisions."

"Sounds like you a few years ago."

More laughter.

"Why do you think I'm spending time with her?"

This time there were oohs and awes.

"Okay, what are some of the things you could do to cut the time you spend with her by 75% without compromising her growth and development?"

Bob dramatized his pensive moments to the amusement of the group before he responded. "Well, I suppose I could share some of the mentoring with you and others."

"Good, I'd be happy to help. What else?"

"I could probably send her to some seminars on strategic management and industry fundamentals, as long as she doesn't fall for some surrogate religion."

Laughter all around.

"What else?"

"Isn't that enough?"

"No."

"You're tough."

"That's what the Results Dialogue is designed to do—push the envelope on solutions."

"Okay. I could probably get my entire team to own this issue because all of them have the same issue in one way or another."

"Bingo," Will said. "Oftentimes, the best solutions emerge after you've gotten past the obvious ones. Let me say that again. The best solutions usually emerge after you've gotten past the obvious ones. But that only happens when you stay engaged in the Results Dialogue. You have to get outside the box, beyond the obvious, and into real creative and critical thinking. Getting Bob's entire team to take greater ownership for this issue is potentially a great solution. The key to realizing results is getting everyone in the organization finding solutions to the issues, problems, and obstacles standing in our way. Clarity around Required Results and Reciprocal Results not only makes this possible but inexorable. Inexorable cultures are the best cultures. What does that mean? If you talk about results everyday with the intent to keep realization of those results on path, it quickly becomes the dominant norm of your culture."

"Am I done?" Bob asked.

"Only if you're ready to implement a solution."

"I'm so ready."

The room burst into laughter again.

"Seriously, what would you need to do to implement a solution?"

"I'd have to write it down, get Sarah's buy-in, start implementing, and then go to the rest of the team with it when we're achieving movement."

"Yes." *All right, they're ready.*

To facilitate their practicing, Barrington's leaders were given 4 x 6-inch Results Dialogue cards with individual questions on one side and group questions on the other. Helping them to effectively use this card in various scenarios similar to the role play with Bob was what Will emphasized for the rest of the afternoon.

At the conclusion of the session, Ann made it clear that each of the leaders whose direct reports were not in the room would be responsible for implementing these same three workshops in their own teams.

"And Will is more than willing to help you."

The ensuing applause was another sign of their energy and readiness.

Going forward, the overall plan was for every Barrington employee to go through some form of level appropriate training in each of the three areas—Required Results, Reciprocal Results, and Realized Results—by the end of July. Each of Ann's direct reports would develop their own implementation plans for their vertical organizations. There was still a lot of work to be done, but this group was on its way.

Finally, a follow-up meeting with the top fifty leaders in the room was scheduled for sixty days out to ensure that everyone was effectively implementing the principles and practices related to creating a Results Revolution at Barrington Corp. A series of pulse surveys would be initiated to begin tracking 90% active involvement of the fifty leaders in the Results Revolution.

Ann Strong concluded their final session with these words, "These three days that we have spent together are going to change everything at Barrington and I could not be prouder of this group for unfreezing your mindsets, suspending your beliefs, staying engaged, and passionately committing to this Results Revolution. It's time to make the bread. Who will help me?"

"We will!" the group shouted as the house came down in a standing ovation.

Traction.

17

RESULTS REVOLUTION UNDERWAY

During the next sixty days, each of the leaders whose direct reports were not in the three sessions in May took their own teams and the next layer of managers through the same three days of training with help from Will and a group of certified internal trainers. The impact on the company was both transformative and surprising.

Most of the five hundred managers and supervisors who attended the next round of workshops couldn't believe it was actually happening at Barrington Corp. Nonetheless, they embraced Barrington's new focus on results with excitement, engagement, and a genuine resolve to change the company's work environment. Aided by strong examples from 90% of the company's top fifty leaders, this second wave of managers from the next two levels of the organizational hierarchy brought an immediate, tangible turnaround in company morale and real movement toward delivering the full suite of Required and Reciprocal Results.

By the end of the year, all 30,000 employees had been through a level-appropriate live or digital version of the Required Results, Reciprocal Results, and Realized Results training. The 12,000 salaried employees attended three full days of workshops similar to what the top fifty leaders experienced. The company's 18,000 hourly workers attended weekly two-hour workshops for eight consecutive weeks or participated in a self-paced digital learning program over the same time period. The two-word phrase "Results Revolution" with its subset of double 'R's—Required Results, Reciprocal Results, and Realized Results—were now on everyone's lips and minds at Barrington. In fact, the *less than 130 words* mantra created in the first workshop by one of the breakout groups had become the company chant:

Profitable Growth, 15 & 20

- If we *don't* grow at 15 and 20, we won't have any bonuses, options, promotions, new products, new services, new customers, satisfied customers, engaged employees, happy shareholders, and opportunities for everyone.

- If we *do* grow at 15 and 20, we will have plenty.

Results Revolution, 90% active involvement

- Join the Results Revolution or lose freedom, opportunity, and money. We must learn how to deliver the Required Results, year in and year out.

- Now, you get to choose—90% in to win.

Market Leadership, 1-2-3 or out

- If we *don't* lead our markets, we'll become knock-off targets.
- If we *do* lead our markets, we'll become attracting magnets of talent, customers, investors, suppliers, vendors, acquisitions, deals, media, and more.

However, it took Barrington Corp twelve more months, almost twenty-one months after the first Results Revolution workshop, to successfully deliver on the company's four Required Results. It also took three more divestitures, four more acquisitions, 1,000 terminations, 3,000 new hires, and a replacement of eight of the company's top fifty leaders.

When the Required Results and Reciprocal Results became Realized Results, there was a huge company party to celebrate both the company's remarkable success and the largest payout in bonuses and stock options in company history.

Results at the organization, team, position, and personal levels were achieved in abundance—over 95% achievement at all levels. The Results Dialogue became the heart of the Results Revolution, just as Jack Grossman had predicted. Those individuals and teams that did not deliver on their Required or Reciprocal Results were given a portion of the benefits the others received.

As a result of the results achieved, the company's stock price soared beyond its previous high of $119 to over $150 per share. Ann Strong was heralded on Wall Street as a turnaround genius and Will Wright was back at the Harvard Business School teaching another inspiring business case, *The Barrington Corporation Turnaround*. Jack Grossman, Bob Daringer, and the other seven members of Ann's senior team were performing brilliantly and loving the bread making.

By all accounts inside and outside the company, Barrington was well on its way to industry dominance and economic leadership. Rogers Barrington was not only ecstatic, he'd also gotten used to spending more time at his villa on St. Bart's in the Caribbean. His doctors, surprised that his heart disease was still non-threatening, were now adding years to their prognosis. In his now frequent interviews with the business media, he was fond of describing Barrington's success as "A Red Hen Revolution." The ensuing questions, of course, allowed him to elaborate in detail. He was thoroughly enjoying life as Chairman of the Board and looked ten years younger. *Grandpa would be able to really rest in peace and maybe, just maybe he'd even be proud.*

A true Results Revolution was underway at The Barrington Corporation with leaders and employees taking on a whole new level of ownership, performance, growth, and passionate bread making. And the legendary fable of The Little Red Hen was being told and retold inside and outside the company.

Long live the Barrington Corporation and the legacy of the little red hen.

18

ASSESSING
YOUR RESULTS

We suggest you take this assessment after you read this book's first seventeen chapters.

Applying the principles of a Results Revolution in your team and organization begins with assessing where you are now. In other words, how do you rate your team's and your organization's current effectiveness and performance relative to:

- Required Results—with its ongoing intense clarification to drive focus;
- Reciprocal Results—with its essential and genuine mutual benefit to drive energy; and

- Realized Results—with its constant dialogue and adjustment to drive solutions.

You can rate your team's and organization's effectiveness and performance by answering the 20 Questions below (use the 1 to 10 scale to answer, 10 being the most positive/favorable answer and 1 being the most negative/unfavorable answer). However, before you answer the 20 Questions, answer five preliminary questions:

A. Can you identify your organization's top four results? If yes, write them down and then discuss them with your boss.
Yes or No

1._____
2._____
3._____
4._____

B. Can you identify your team's top four results? (This is the team you are a member of.) If yes, same as above.
Yes or No

1._____
2._____
3._____
4._____

C. Can you identify your team's top four results? (This is the team you lead.) If yes, same as above.
Yes or No

1._____
2._____
3._____
4._____

D. Are your teams' top four results directly linked to the organization's top four results? Yes or No

E. Are you and your team genuinely enthusiastic about and persistent in pursuing the organization's top four results? Yes or No

F. Do you always know when you are meeting or exceeding your results? Yes or No

Two or more "No" answers to the five preliminary questions indicate the need for a Results Revolution. Now, answer the 20 Questions to further clarify your needs:

1. How clearly defined and understood are your organization's top 3-5 key results?

    1   2   3   4   5   6   7   8   9   10

2. Do your organization's top 3-5 key results reflect what "matters most" to your team and the organization's success?

    1   2   3   4   5   6   7   8   9   10

3. Are your organization's top 3-5 key results strategically critical, organizationally meaningful, and operationally measureable?

    1   2   3   4   5   6   7   8   9   10

4. Do your team's top 3-5 key results clearly and efficiently tie to the organization's top 3-5 key results?

    1   2   3   4   5   6   7   8   9   10

5. Has each member of your team clearly defined 3-5 key results for their respective positions (and teams) and adequately tied them to the organization's top 3-5 key results?

    1   2   3   4   5   6   7   8   9   10

6. Do you frequently monitor and communicate progress toward achieving organization, team, and position key results?

    1   2   3   4   5   6   7   8   9   10

7. Has every member of your team clearly defined 3-5 personal and professional key results for himself or herself?

    1   2   3   4   5   6   7   8   9   10

8. Do your own 3-5 personal and professional key results reflect what "matters most" to you at this stage in your career/life?

    1   2   3   4   5   6   7   8   9   10

9. Do the top 3-5 personal and professional key results identified by you and your team members reflect what "matters most" to your and their success?

    1   2   3   4   5   6   7   8   9   10

10. Are you fully aware of the top 3-5 personal and professional key results desired by each member of your team?

    1   2   3   4   5   6   7   8   9   10

11. Are you fully aware of the top 3-5 personal and professional key results desired by your boss?

    1   2   3   4   5   6   7   8   9   10

12. Do you frequently discuss progress toward achieving the top 3-5 personal and professional key results with other members of your team?

    1   2   3   4   5   6   7   8   9   10

13. Are you having results conversations on a daily basis with your boss, your peers, and/or your direct reports?

    1   2   3   4   5   6   7   8   9   10

14. During your results conversations do you address gaps and find solutions?

    1   2   3   4   5   6   7   8   9   10

15. Do you constantly work to keep your primary focus on achieving the top 3-5 key results for the organization, team, position and personally/professionally?

    1   2   3   4   5   6   7   8   9   10

16. Are you actively conversational about your team members' motivations and energy levels relative to delivering the needed results?

 1 2 3 4 5 6 7 8 9 10

17. Are you and your team members actively engaged in finding the necessary solutions to achieve organization, team, position and personal/professional top 3-5 key results?

 1 2 3 4 5 6 7 8 9 10

18. Are you and your team members relentless in your efforts to ensure that your team's top 3-5 key results are realized?

 1 2 3 4 5 6 7 8 9 10

19. What percentage of your time (10 = 100%) do you spend on achieving the organization's top 3-5 key results?

 1 2 3 4 5 6 7 8 9 10

20. What percentage of your team's time (10 = 100%) is spent on achieving the organization's top 3-5 key results?

 1 2 3 4 5 6 7 8 9 10

To complete your assessment, add your scores on the 20 Questions together to come up with a total score. A total score of 160 or below indicates the need for a Results Revolution in your team and organization.

In order to identify where your current need is greatest:

- Add your scores to questions 1 through 6 to obtain a subtotal score for Required Results.
- Add your scores to questions 7 through 12 to obtain a subtotal score for Reciprocal Results.

- Add your scores to questions 13 through 18 to obtain a subtotal score for Realized Results.

      Whichever subtotal score is lowest indicates the "Results" area where your team or organization is currently in most need of improvement.

      Complete the table on the following page to summarize the current state of your results.

State of Your Team's & Organization's Results	Total_____out of 200
Required Results	Subtotal_____out of 60
Reciprocal Results	Subtotal_____out of 60
Realized Results	Subtotal_____out of 60

Appendix

RESULTS REVOLUTION LEVERS FOR CHANGE

This Appendix is a summary of the concepts and principles applied to produce Barrington Corp's Results Revolution.

Business Challenge: Results are the key to everything in business. But many business leaders fail to achieve key results in a successful and sustainable manner.

Levers for Change: To better address your business challenges, start using three simple levers—Required Results, Reciprocal Results, Realized Results—to successfully drive greater Focus, Energy and Solutions in your organization. Strategy, leadership and culture are still vitally important to the sustainable success of any business organization, but they must assume their appropriate places and never distract from what matters most (i.e., results), as shown in the model below:

Results Revolution: This transformation process will help you overcome the distractions inherent in strategy, leadership, and culture to achieve what matters most for yourself, your team, and your organization—now and going forward.

Three Days That Change Everything: The three workshops described in this book are three days of intervention (or the equivalent in digital learning experiences) designed to launch a Results Revolution. Day 1 is focused on Required Results, Day 2 on Reciprocal Results, and Day 3 on Realized Results. To achieve maximum impact, every team in the organization, beginning with the senior team, should experience these three days in one form or another. However, if the entire organization is not involved in the Results Revolution, individual divisions, business units, functions, departments, or middle management and lower level teams can derive great benefit from this transformation process. Results Revolutions advance one team at a time.

Next Steps: There are two questions to address and discuss at this point: 1) What is the Return on Investment of a Results Revolution? and 2) Where do we start and with which Team(s)? Our client service consultants will be happy to help you answer these questions and more.

Partners In Leadership
27555 Ynez Road, Suite 300
Temecula CA 92590
www.partnersinleadership.com
800-504-6070

ABOUT THE AUTHORS

CRAIG HICKMAN has authored 17 books, among them such international bestsellers as T*he Oz Principle*, *Creating Excellence*, *Mind of a Manager Soul of a Leader*, *The Strategy Game*, *Fix It*, and *The Insiders*. He is a Harvard MBA with honors, former CEO of Headwaters Technology Innovation (HW:NYSE), founder of the consulting firm Management Perspectives Group, and currently Futurist and SVP of New Product Development at Partners In Leadership, the premier provider of Accountability and Culture Change services worldwide. His clients include many of the Fortune 1000 companies. He lives in Temecula, CA.

CRAIG MORGAN is a talent management and leadership development consultant, practitioner, thought leader, and former executive. He has spent 30 years driving results and raising the bar of performance with small to Fortune 50 companies. With master's degrees in Organizational Transformation from Columbia, DePaul, and the Jungian Institute, he ran a national award-winning corporate university for Neumann Homes and led Organizational Development and Effectiveness for Occidental Petroleum (OXY:NYSE) and RR Donnelley(RRD:NYSE). He is founder of The Gray Matter Advantage, a performance management practice, and a consultant to Partners In Leadership. He lives in Chicago, IL.

Partners In Leadership guides clients in defining Key Results™, shaping Cultural Beliefs©, and solving Accountability Gaps. With our network of experts around the world and #1 award-winning content, we help clients achieve their mission by dramatically boosting employee engagement, inspiring innovation, improving cross-collaboration, developing accountable leaders, blending strategy with culture, and more.

 Partners In Leadership®

partnersinleadership.com
800.504.6070